"After utilizing toolkits from The Art of Service, I was able to identify threats within my organization to which I was completely unaware. Using my team's knowledge as a competitive advantage, we now have superior systems that save time and energy."

"As a new Chief Technology Officer, I was feeling unprepared and inadequate to be successful in my role. I ordered an IT toolkit Sunday night and was prepared Monday morning to shed light on areas of improvement within my organization. I no longer felt overwhelmed and intimidated, I was excited to share what I had learned."

"I used the questionnaires to interview members of my team. I never knew how many insights we could produce collectively with our internal knowledge."

"I usually work until at least 8pm on weeknights. The Art of Service questionnaire saved me so much time and worry that Thursday night I attended my son's soccer game without sacrificing my professional obligations."

"After purchasing The Art of Service toolkit, I was able to identify areas where my company was not in compliance that could have put my job at risk. I looked like a hero when I proactively educated my team on the risks and presented a solid solution."

"I spent months shopping for an external consultant before realizing that The Art of Service would allow my team to consult themselves! Not only did we save time not catching a consultant up to speed, we were able to keep our company information and industry secrets confidential."

"Everyday there are new regulations and processes in my industry. The Art of Service toolkit has kept me ahead by using AI technology to constantly update the toolkits and address emerging needs."

"I customized The Art of Service toolkit to focus specifically on the concerns of my role and industry. I didn't have to waste time with a generic self-help book that wasn't tailored to my exact situation."

"Many of our competitors have asked us about our secret sauce. When I tell them it's the knowledge we have in-house, they never believe me. Little do they know The Art of Service toolkits are working behind the scenes."

"One of my friends hired a consultant who used the knowledge gained working with his company to advise their competitor. Talk about a competitive disadvantage! The Art of Service allowed us to keep our knowledge from walking out the door along with a huge portion of our budget in consulting fees."

"Honestly, I didn't know what I didn't know. Before purchasing The Art of Service, I didn't realize how many areas of my business needed to be refreshed and improved. I am so relieved The Art of Service was there to highlight our blind spots."

"Before The Art of Service, I waited eagerly for consulting company reports to come out each month. These reports kept us up to speed but provided little value because they put our competitors on the same playing field. With The Art of Service, we have uncovered unique insights to drive our business forward."

"Instead of investing extensive resources into an external consultant, we can spend more of our budget towards pursuing our company goals and objectives...while also spending a little more on corporate holiday parties."

"The risk of our competitors getting ahead has been mitigated because The Art of Service has provided us with a 360-degree view of threats within our organization before they even arise."

Supplier Quality Management
Complete Self-Assessment Guide

https://theartofservice.com
support@theartofservice.com

Table of Contents

About The Art of Service

The Art of Service, Business Process Architects since 2000, is dedicated to helping stakeholders achieve excellence.

Defining, designing, creating, and implementing a process to solve a stakeholders challenge or meet an objective is the most valuable role… In EVERY group, company, organization and department.

Unless you're talking a one-time, single-use project, there should be a process. Whether that process is managed and implemented by humans, AI, or a combination of the two, it needs to be designed by someone with a complex enough perspective to ask the right questions.

Someone capable of asking the right questions and step back and say, 'What are we really trying to accomplish here? And is there a different way to look at it?'

With The Art of Service's Self-Assessments, we empower people who can do just that — whether their title is marketer, entrepreneur, manager, salesperson, consultant, Business Process Manager, executive assistant, IT Manager, CIO etc... —they are the people who rule the future. They are people who watch the process as it happens, and ask the right questions to make the process work better.

Contact us when you need any support with this Self-Assessment and any help with templates, blue-prints and examples of standard documents you might need:

https://theartofservice.com
support@theartofservice.com

Included Resources - how to access

Included with your purchase of the book is the Supplier Quality

Management Self-Assessment Spreadsheet Dashboard which contains all questions and Self-Assessment areas and auto-generates insights, graphs, and project RACI planning - all with examples to get you started right away.

How? Simply send an email to
access@theartofservice.com
with this books' title in the subject to get the Supplier Quality Management Self Assessment Tool right away.

The auto reply will guide you further, you will then receive the following contents with New and Updated specific criteria:

- The latest quick edition of the book in PDF
- The latest complete edition of the book in PDF, which criteria correspond to the criteria in...
- The Self-Assessment Excel Dashboard, and...
- Example pre-filled Self-Assessment Excel Dashboard to get familiar with results generation
- In-depth specific Checklists covering the topic
- Project management checklists and templates to assist with implementation

INCLUDES LIFETIME SELF ASSESSMENT UPDATES

Every self assessment comes with Lifetime Updates and Lifetime Free Updated Books. Lifetime Updates is an industry-first feature which allows you to receive verified self assessment updates, ensuring you always have the most accurate information at your fingertips.

Get it now- you will be glad you did - do it now, before you forget.

Send an email to **access@theartofservice.com** with this books' title in the subject to get the Supplier Quality Management Self Assessment Tool right away.

Purpose of this Self-Assessment

This Self-Assessment has been developed to improve understanding of the requirements and elements of Supplier Quality Management, based on best practices and standards in business process architecture, design and quality management.

It is designed to allow for a rapid Self-Assessment to determine how closely existing management practices and procedures correspond to the elements of the Self-Assessment.

The criteria of requirements and elements of Supplier Quality Management have been rephrased in the format of a Self-Assessment questionnaire, with a seven-criterion scoring system, as explained in this document.

In this format, even with limited background knowledge of Supplier Quality Management, a manager can quickly review existing operations to determine how they measure up to the standards. This in turn can serve as the starting point of a 'gap analysis' to identify management tools or system elements that might usefully be implemented in the organization to help improve overall performance.

How to use the Self-Assessment

On the following pages are a series of questions to identify to what extent your Supplier Quality Management initiative is complete in comparison to the requirements set in standards.

To facilitate answering the questions, there is a space in front of each question to enter a score on a scale of '1' to '5'.

1 Strongly Disagree

2 Disagree

3 Neutral

4 Agree

5 Strongly Agree

Read the question and rate it with the following in front of mind:

'In my belief, the answer to this question is clearly defined'.

There are two ways in which you can choose to interpret this statement;

1. how aware are you that the answer to the question is clearly defined
2. for more in-depth analysis you can choose to gather evidence and confirm the answer to the question. This obviously will take more time, most Self-Assessment users opt for the first way to interpret the question and dig deeper later on based on the outcome of the overall Self-Assessment.

A score of '1' would mean that the answer is not clear at all, where a '5' would mean the answer is crystal clear and defined. Leave emtpy when the question is not applicable or you don't want to answer it, you can skip it without affecting your score. Write your score in the space provided.

After you have responded to all the appropriate statements in each section, compute your average score for that section, using the formula provided, and round to the nearest tenth. Then transfer to the corresponding spoke in the Supplier Quality Management Scorecard on the second next page of the Self-Assessment.

Your completed Supplier Quality Management Scorecard will give you a clear presentation of which Supplier Quality Management areas need attention.

Supplier Quality Management Scorecard Example

Example of how the finalized Scorecard can look like:

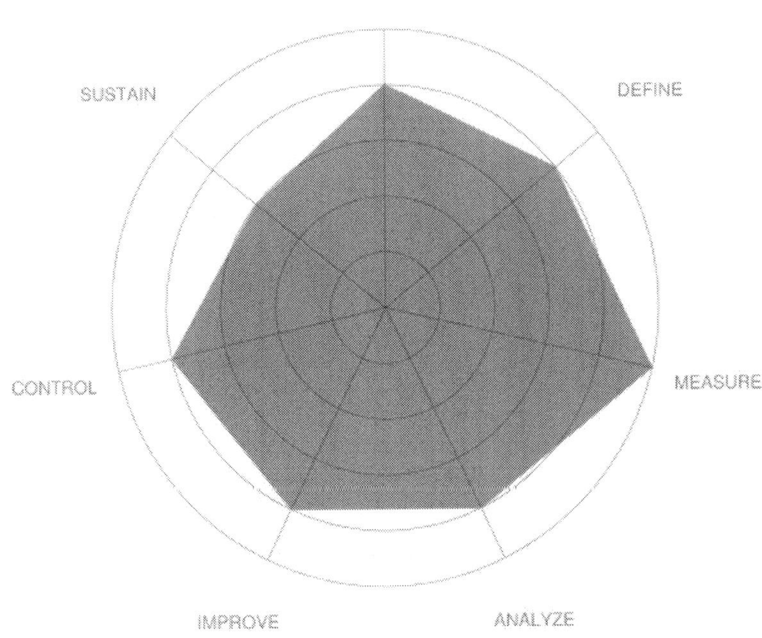

Supplier Quality Management Scorecard

Your Scores:

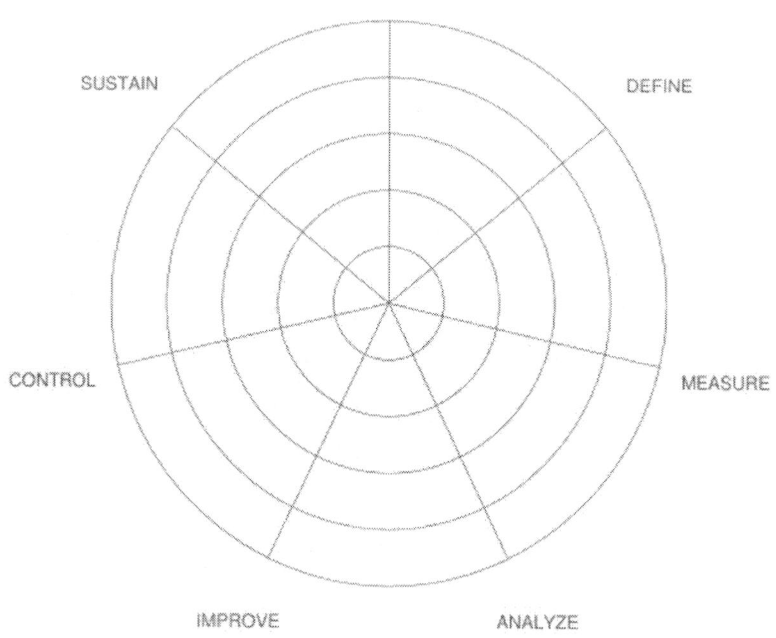

BEGINNING OF THE SELF-ASSESSMENT:

CRITERION #1: RECOGNIZE

INTENT: Be aware of the need for change. Recognize that there is an unfavorable variation, problem or symptom.

In my belief, the answer to this question is clearly defined:

5 Strongly Agree

4 Agree

3 Neutral

2 Disagree

1 Strongly Disagree

1. How much are sponsors, customers, partners, stakeholders involved in Supplier Quality Management? In other words, what are the risks, if Supplier Quality Management does not deliver successfully?
<--- Score

2. Is product inspection status identified?
<--- Score

3. What problems are you facing and how do you consider Supplier Quality Management will circumvent those obstacles?
<--- Score

4. What criteria are used in deciding whether to issue a permit to an individual or your organization?
<--- Score

5. Who is responsible for the accurate identification & traceability of assets & material?
<--- Score

6. What are your needs in relation to Supplier Quality Management skills, labor, equipment, and markets?
<--- Score

7. Is there a procedure for implementing corrective and preventive actions?
<--- Score

8. What is the problem or issue?
<--- Score

9. Have operators basic training needs been fulfilled for the job being performed?
<--- Score

10. Are handling controls adequate to prevent damage and deterioration?
<--- Score

11. What types of assets and material must be individually identified and tracked for quality

purposes?
<--- Score

12. What does Supplier Quality Management success mean to the stakeholders?
<--- Score

13. Are the required instruments and test equipment adequately identified?
<--- Score

14. How capable is your organization at Problem Solving?
<--- Score

15. Does management review corrective and preventive actions?
<--- Score

16. Are corrective and preventive actions retained?
<--- Score

17. How can auditing be a preventative security measure?
<--- Score

18. Are the quality records adequately identified, collected, indexed, filed, stored, maintained and eventually disposed of?
<--- Score

19. Is the effectiveness of corrective or preventive actions verified?
<--- Score

20. Is there any form of automated support for

Issues Management?
<--- Score

21. Have current and future quality issues been identified from the quality records system?
<--- Score

22. How are you going to measure success?
<--- Score

23. Is there a system for assigning responsibility for corrective actions to prevent recurrence?
<--- Score

24. Have the roles and responsibilities of all project members been identified?
<--- Score

25. Is there a formal set of procedures supporting Issues Management?
<--- Score

26. Is there a procedure that defines the marking and identification of non-conforming material?
<--- Score

27. Does your organization determine and manage the work environment needed to achieve conformity to product requirements?
<--- Score

28. How are quality problems reported?
<--- Score

29. What situation(s) led to this Supplier Quality Management Self Assessment?

<--- Score

30. What are the expected benefits of Supplier Quality Management to the stakeholder?
<--- Score

31. Have the scope of work, desired outcomes, budget and key dates for the project been identified?
<--- Score

32. Are there procedures for identifying product from receipt through all stages of production?
<--- Score

33. What are the stakeholder objectives to be achieved with Supplier Quality Management?
<--- Score

34. Is there evidence of a preventive maintenance program?
<--- Score

35. What do you need to start doing?
<--- Score

36. Where are the verification arrangements and method of product release identified?
<--- Score

37. Are the measures to control nonconforming product adequate to prevent inadvertent use or installation?
<--- Score

38. Is the product identified by item and batch, or

lot, during all stages of production, delivery, and installation?
<--- Score

39. Are quality records stored in a suitable manner to prevent deterioration, damage, or loss?
<--- Score

40. Does the supplier clearly identify nonconforming and suspect product and the quarantine areas?
<--- Score

41. As a sponsor, customer or management, how important is it to meet goals, objectives?
<--- Score

42. What would happen if Supplier Quality Management weren't done?
<--- Score

43. Has the supplier appointed a management representative who has unrestricted access to top management to resolve quality issues?
<--- Score

44. Are corrective actions, for any deficiencies identified in an audit, carried out on a timely basis?
<--- Score

45. How do you measure quality issues connected to supplier at the after market?
<--- Score

46. What tools and technologies are needed for a

custom Supplier Quality Management project?
<--- Score

47. Can top management demonstrate that it has provided resources needed for the qms?
<--- Score

48. How do you measure your ability to meet needs and expectations?
<--- Score

49. Have you had any quality problems?
<--- Score

50. Is it needed?
<--- Score

51. Are the supplier Quality records identifiable to the product and the subcontract involved?
<--- Score

52. Does the supplier identify all software Quality activities related to software acceptance testing?
<--- Score

53. Are there any specific expectations or concerns about the Supplier Quality Management team, Supplier Quality Management itself?
<--- Score

54. Are there procedures for identifying training needs for personnel affecting quality?
<--- Score

55. Have you had any problems with the product-quality?

<--- Score

56. Who else hopes to benefit from it?
<--- Score

57. How are the Supplier Quality Management's objectives aligned to the group's overall stakeholder strategy?
<--- Score

58. How do you assess your Supplier Quality Management workforce capability and capacity needs, including skills, competencies, and staffing levels?
<--- Score

59. How many of behaviours do you recognize in your organization?
<--- Score

60. Do you know what you need to know about Supplier Quality Management?
<--- Score

Add up total points for this section:
_____ = Total points for this section

Divided by: ______ (number of statements answered) = ______
Average score for this section

Transfer your score to the Supplier Quality Management Index at the beginning of the Self-Assessment.

CRITERION #2: DEFINE:

INTENT: Formulate the stakeholder problem. Define the problem, needs and objectives.

In my belief, the answer to this question is clearly defined:

5 Strongly Agree

4 Agree

3 Neutral

2 Disagree

1 Strongly Disagree

1. What are the compelling stakeholder reasons for embarking on Supplier Quality Management?
<--- Score

2. Do you flow down quality requirements to your suppliers?
<--- Score

3. If substitutes have been appointed, have they

been briefed on the Supplier Quality Management goals and received regular communications as to the progress to date?
<--- Score

4. Do the problem and goal statements meet the SMART criteria (specific, measurable, attainable, relevant, and time-bound)?
<--- Score

5. Has the direction changed at all during the course of Supplier Quality Management? If so, when did it change and why?
<--- Score

6. Are customer(s) identified and segmented according to their different needs and requirements?
<--- Score

7. Are different versions of process maps needed to account for the different types of inputs?
<--- Score

8. How often are the team meetings?
<--- Score

9. Does your organizations top management ensure that the responsibilities and authorities are defined and communicated within your organization?
<--- Score

10. Do you maintain an approved supplier list that includes the scope of the approval?
<--- Score

11. Is the Supplier Quality Management scope manageable?
<--- Score

12. When is/was the Supplier Quality Management start date?
<--- Score

13. How are requirements determined?
<--- Score

14. How are post delivery requirements met?
<--- Score

15. Has the Supplier Quality Management work been fairly and/or equitably divided and delegated among team members who are qualified and capable to perform the work? Has everyone contributed?
<--- Score

16. What knowledge or experience is required?
<--- Score

17. How do you build the right business case?
<--- Score

18. Has the improvement team collected the 'voice of the customer' (obtained feedback – qualitative and quantitative)?
<--- Score

19. How does the Supplier Quality Management manager ensure against scope creep?
<--- Score

20. Does the team have regular meetings?

<--- Score

21. What are the rough order estimates on cost savings/opportunities that Supplier Quality Management brings?
<--- Score

22. Is full participation by members in regularly held team meetings guaranteed?
<--- Score

23. Is Supplier Quality Management currently on schedule according to the plan?
<--- Score

24. Do you comply with requirements?
<--- Score

25. When is the estimated completion date?
<--- Score

26. Should consultants be used to define and implement change?
<--- Score

27. Are stakeholder processes mapped?
<--- Score

28. Has a high-level 'as is' process map been completed, verified and validated?
<--- Score

29. Do your purchase orders adequately flow down your requirements to your suppliers?
<--- Score

30. Is the team equipped with available and reliable resources?
<--- Score

31. Do suppliers of your materials have to meet specific environmental requirements?
<--- Score

32. Is the team sponsored by a champion or stakeholder leader?
<--- Score

33. What sources do you use to gather information for a Supplier Quality Management study?
<--- Score

34. Do retained quality records demonstrate conformance to product requirements?
<--- Score

35. How does your organization gather quality feedback from the customers?
<--- Score

36. Is there a critical path to deliver Supplier Quality Management results?
<--- Score

37. How to define team for pay purposes?
<--- Score

38. What Supplier Quality Management requirements should be gathered?
<--- Score

39. Is a fully trained team formed, supported,

and committed to work on the Supplier Quality Management improvements?
<--- Score

40. Are the required equipment and/or services available from more than one supplier?
<--- Score

41. Is there regularly 100% attendance at the team meetings? If not, have appointed substitutes attended to preserve cross-functionality and full representation?
<--- Score

42. Have the customer needs been translated into specific, measurable requirements? How?
<--- Score

43. What sort of initial information to gather?
<--- Score

44. What level of training is required to use the custom reporting engine?
<--- Score

45. What are the external quality requirements?
<--- Score

46. Are improvement team members fully trained on Supplier Quality Management?
<--- Score

47. Do you maintain records to demonstrate conformance to specified requirements?
<--- Score

48. Has everyone on the team, including the team leaders, been properly trained?
<--- Score

49. What are the top IIoT use cases your organization will start pursuing in the next year?
<--- Score

50. Have audit criteria, scope, frequency and methods been defined?
<--- Score

51. Are there quality assurance requirements?
<--- Score

52. What are the boundaries of the scope? What is in bounds and what is not? What is the start point? What is the stop point?
<--- Score

53. Have organizational requirements been reviewed to determine diversity in the workforce?
<--- Score

54. How are customers product and service requirements determined and reviewed?
<--- Score

55. Are team charters developed?
<--- Score

56. Is the work to date meeting requirements?
<--- Score

57. What is the scope?
<--- Score

58. How do you assure that your sub suppliers are complying with your requirements?
<--- Score

59. Is data collected and displayed to better understand customer(s) critical needs and requirements.
<--- Score

60. How are consistent Supplier Quality Management definitions important?
<--- Score

61. What are the key elements required in order to assure a smooth and successful implementation?
<--- Score

62. Are records maintained for product acceptance to purchase order / customer requirements?
<--- Score

63. Are design input parameters adequately defined?
<--- Score

64. Does your organization define quality according to performance?
<--- Score

65. What would be the goal or target for a Supplier Quality Management's improvement team?
<--- Score

66. What are the Roles and Responsibilities for each team member and its leadership? Where is this

documented?
<--- Score

67. How was the 'as is' process map developed, reviewed, verified and validated?
<--- Score

68. How did the Supplier Quality Management manager receive input to the development of a Supplier Quality Management improvement plan and the estimated completion dates/times of each activity?
<--- Score

69. Is there a completed SIPOC representation, describing the Suppliers, Inputs, Process, Outputs, and Customers?
<--- Score

70. Do you have organizational privacy requirements?
<--- Score

71. Is there a completed, verified, and validated high-level 'as is' (not 'should be' or 'could be') stakeholder process map?
<--- Score

72. Are customer satisfaction surveys conducted in periodical manner as required?
<--- Score

73. Has anyone else (internal or external to the group) attempted to solve this problem or a similar one before? If so, what knowledge can be leveraged from these previous efforts?
<--- Score

74. Will team members perform Supplier Quality Management work when assigned and in a timely fashion?
<--- Score

75. Does the quality system define what constitutes executive responsibility?
<--- Score

76. Do you all define Supplier Quality Management in the same way?
<--- Score

77. Is Supplier Quality Management linked to key stakeholder goals and objectives?
<--- Score

78. Are there different segments of customers?
<--- Score

79. Has your organization defined the scope of the QMS?
<--- Score

80. What are the dynamics of the communication plan?
<--- Score

81. Is the improvement team aware of the different versions of a process: what they think it is vs. what it actually is vs. what it should be vs. what it could be?
<--- Score

82. Which requirements changed since the last customer review?

<--- Score

83. Will team members regularly document their Supplier Quality Management work?
<--- Score

84. How do you manage unclear Supplier Quality Management requirements?
<--- Score

85. How do you keep key subject matter experts in the loop?
<--- Score

86. How have you defined all Supplier Quality Management requirements first?
<--- Score

87. Do companies require specification of the quality of input materials?
<--- Score

88. Has a team charter been developed and communicated?
<--- Score

89. What critical content must be communicated – who, what, when, where, and how?
<--- Score

90. What constraints exist that might impact the team?
<--- Score

91. How will the Supplier Quality Management team and the group measure complete success of Supplier

Quality Management?
<--- Score

92. Are there procedures that define how customer supplied products and equipment are controlled and maintained?
<--- Score

93. When are meeting minutes sent out? Who is on the distribution list?
<--- Score

94. What quality requirements do you have of your suppliers?
<--- Score

95. Do you have a function that reviews purchasing requirements to ensure that the material purchased meets customer requirements?
<--- Score

96. What key stakeholder process output measure(s) does Supplier Quality Management leverage and how?
<--- Score

97. Are there any constraints known that bear on the ability to perform Supplier Quality Management work? How is the team addressing them?
<--- Score

98. What customer feedback methods were used to solicit their input?
<--- Score

99. Are records available for review by customers

and regulatory authorities in accordance with contract or regulatory requirements?
<--- Score

100. Are customers identified and high impact areas defined?
<--- Score

101. How is the team tracking and documenting its work?
<--- Score

102. Is there a clear Supplier Quality Management case definition?
<--- Score

103. Is the current 'as is' process being followed? If not, what are the discrepancies?
<--- Score

104. Has/have the customer(s) been identified?
<--- Score

105. Are there any environmental or make good requirements?
<--- Score

106. Do you meet all the requirements?
<--- Score

107. Is the team formed and are team leaders (Coaches and Management Leads) assigned?
<--- Score

108. What are the top IIoT use cases your organization is pursuing today?

<--- Score

109. Are the procedures to execute the maintenance of the production equipment defined?
<--- Score

110. Do you perform inspection and testing to ensure compliance to customer requirements?
<--- Score

111. What specifically is the problem? Where does it occur? When does it occur? What is its extent?
<--- Score

112. Is the authority and reporting responsibility of the Quality Manager clearly defined?
<--- Score

113. Who are the Supplier Quality Management improvement team members, including Management Leads and Coaches?
<--- Score

114. Has a project plan, Gantt chart, or similar been developed/completed?
<--- Score

115. Is there a Supplier Quality Management management charter, including stakeholder case, problem and goal statements, scope, milestones, roles and responsibilities, communication plan?
<--- Score

116. How does your organization gather quality feedback from customers?

<--- Score

117. How will variation in the actual durations of each activity be dealt with to ensure that the expected Supplier Quality Management results are met?
<--- Score

118. Does the quality policy include commitment to satisfy requirements?
<--- Score

119. Is the team adequately staffed with the desired cross-functionality? If not, what additional resources are available to the team?
<--- Score

Add up total points for this section:
_____ = Total points for this section

Divided by: ______ (number of statements answered) = ______
Average score for this section

Transfer your score to the Supplier Quality Management Index at the beginning of the Self-Assessment.

CRITERION #3: MEASURE:

INTENT: Gather the correct data. Measure the current performance and evolution of the situation.

In my belief, the answer to this question is clearly defined:

5 Strongly Agree

4 Agree

3 Neutral

2 Disagree

1 Strongly Disagree

1. Are records kept to indicate evidence of calibration for all measurement equipment used that could affect product quality?
<--- Score

2. Are there any complex design features that present a particular cause for concern?
<--- Score

3. Is Process Variation Displayed/Communicated?
<--- Score

4. Has the impact or consequence of the given risk occurring been assessed?
<--- Score

5. Does management have the right priorities among projects?
<--- Score

6. Are calibration records maintained for all measurement equipment?
<--- Score

7. Which benchmarks does your organization use to measure quality?
<--- Score

8. Are potential consequences / risks documented and analyzed prior to applying the changes?
<--- Score

9. What charts has the team used to display the components of variation in the process?
<--- Score

10. How will measures be used to manage and adapt?
<--- Score

11. What has the team done to assure the stability and accuracy of the measurement process?
<--- Score

12. Is data collected on key measures that were identified?

<--- Score

13. When do you measure supplier performance?
<--- Score

14. How does blockchain impact quality?
<--- Score

15. How do you do risk analysis of rare, cascading, catastrophic events?
<--- Score

16. Which metrics do you use to measure supplier performance?
<--- Score

17. Are key measures identified and agreed upon?
<--- Score

18. What data was collected (past, present, future/ongoing)?
<--- Score

19. Is long term and short term variability accounted for?
<--- Score

20. Is quality, cost and content of work products adequate?
<--- Score

21. Does the measure include milestones and or indicators to express qualitative criteria?
<--- Score

22. What key measures identified indicate the

performance of the stakeholder process?
<--- Score

23. Does Supplier Quality Management systematically track and analyze outcomes for accountability and quality improvement?
<--- Score

24. What is the Supplier Quality Management business impact?
<--- Score

25. What are your key Supplier Quality Management organizational performance measures, including key short and longer-term financial measures?
<--- Score

26. Have design-to-cost goals been established?
<--- Score

27. What business consequences have resulted from weak or ineffective focus on Quality management functions?
<--- Score

28. How do you verify your resources?
<--- Score

29. Are there documented procedures to control and verify the design of your products?
<--- Score

30. Is there a documented system for performing, verifying and reporting servicing as required by contractual or regulatory requirements?
<--- Score

31. What are the agreed upon definitions of the high impact areas, defect(s), unit(s), and opportunities that will figure into the process capability metrics?
<--- Score

32. What is the project likely to cost?
<--- Score

33. How is data analyzed and evaluated?
<--- Score

34. Do the analysts and supervisor know the archiving schedule for filters?
<--- Score

35. How large is the gap between current performance and the customer-specified (goal) performance?
<--- Score

36. Are there documented procedures for identifying the causes of nonconforming product?
<--- Score

37. Are records of nonconforming product, of the causes, and of the corrective actions taken, adequately maintained?
<--- Score

38. Has your organization developed and deployed secure mobile, Cloud and analytics strategies to enter the next generation of predictive analytics?
<--- Score

39. What is the impact if change is disapproved?
<--- Score

40. Have you found any 'ground fruit' or 'low-hanging fruit' for immediate remedies to the gap in performance?
<--- Score

41. How do you identify and analyze stakeholders and their interests?
<--- Score

42. How is the quality of the measures ensured?
<--- Score

43. Have you made assumptions about the shape of the future, particularly its impact on your customers and competitors?
<--- Score

44. Are Supplier Quality Management vulnerabilities categorized and prioritized?
<--- Score

45. What type of out-of-the-box business analytics are provided?
<--- Score

46. What is the project likely to cost considering schedule to date more than cost to date?
<--- Score

47. Is there a Performance Baseline?
<--- Score

48. How does top management demonstrate

customer focus?
<--- Score

49. What will the remaining work cost?
<--- Score

50. Is data collection planned and executed?
<--- Score

51. When a disaster occurs, who gets priority?
<--- Score

52. Are you maximizing working capital costs while also improving material quality and scheduling?
<--- Score

53. Was a business case (cost/benefit) developed?
<--- Score

54. Who should receive measurement reports?
<--- Score

55. What are some tools and methods used to analyze and improve work processes?
<--- Score

56. Does the Supplier Quality Management task fit the client's priorities?
<--- Score

57. What particular quality tools did the team find helpful in establishing measurements?
<--- Score

58. Are you able to realize any cost savings?

<--- Score

59. How do you measure the value of relationships?
<--- Score

60. What users will be impacted?
<--- Score

61. Who participated in the data collection for measurements?
<--- Score

62. What is the nature of change on which the medium sized organization can focus?
<--- Score

63. What are the costs of lack of quality?
<--- Score

64. Will your organization focus on reducing cost or maximizing value?
<--- Score

65. What are the operational costs after Supplier Quality Management deployment?
<--- Score

66. Is key measure data collection planned and executed, process variation displayed and communicated and performance baselined?
<--- Score

67. How are costs allocated?
<--- Score

68. Are actual costs in line with budgeted costs?
<--- Score

69. How do you measure variability?
<--- Score

70. Are process variation components displayed/ communicated using suitable charts, graphs, plots?
<--- Score

71. Was a data collection plan established?
<--- Score

72. Are high impact defects defined and identified in the stakeholder process?
<--- Score

73. What are the key input variables? What are the key process variables? What are the key output variables?
<--- Score

74. Is a solid data collection plan established that includes measurement systems analysis?
<--- Score

75. Can you measure the return on analysis?
<--- Score

76. How do you verify the Supplier Quality Management requirements quality?
<--- Score

77. How your organization satisfies its customers and measures the satisfaction?
<--- Score

78. How long to keep data and how to manage retention costs?
<--- Score

Add up total points for this section:
_____ = Total points for this section

Divided by: ______ (number of statements answered) = ______ Average score for this section

Transfer your score to the Supplier Quality Management Index at the beginning of the Self-Assessment.

CRITERION #4: ANALYZE:

INTENT: Analyze causes, assumptions and hypotheses.

In my belief, the answer to this question is clearly defined:

5 Strongly Agree

4 Agree

3 Neutral

2 Disagree

1 Strongly Disagree

1. Is incoming product subject to inspection prior to being released to processing or storage?
<--- Score

2. Were there any improvement opportunities identified from the process analysis?
<--- Score

3. Are all staff in core Supplier Quality Management subjects Highly Qualified?

<--- Score

4. Are the design and development activities conducted among the relevant groups that should have input to the design process?
<--- Score

5. Are processes operated/performed by qualified employees?
<--- Score

6. Where are manufacturing process design input requirements documented?
<--- Score

7. How does your application allow for easy adoption and simplified processes?
<--- Score

8. What process should you select for improvement?
<--- Score

9. How are nonconforming outputs controlled?
<--- Score

10. Is there a process for addressing suspect counterfeit parts?
<--- Score

11. What is the backup and recovery process?
<--- Score

12. Is data and process analysis, root cause analysis and quantifying the gap/opportunity in place?
<--- Score

13. What systems/processes must you excel at?
<--- Score

14. What are the Supplier Quality Management business drivers?
<--- Score

15. How do your work systems and key work processes relate to and capitalize on your core competencies?
<--- Score

16. What data do you need to collect?
<--- Score

17. Does the software Quality program assure process and product nonconformances are?
<--- Score

18. Have all processes affecting product/service quality been identified and controlled?
<--- Score

19. Is the vendors software / hardware design process documented?
<--- Score

20. Does the configuration Management Process Include?
<--- Score

21. Is there a process for establishment, implementation and maintenance of Design and Development activities?
<--- Score

22. Was a cause-and-effect diagram used to explore the different types of causes (or sources of variation)?
<--- Score

23. Is the process for each feature in control, stable and normally distributed?
<--- Score

24. How do you document your risk management process and prove it in an audit?
<--- Score

25. Are gaps between current performance and the goal performance identified?
<--- Score

26. What are the qualification details for suppliers by top purchase order amount?
<--- Score

27. What is the process improvement cycle?
<--- Score

28. Has communication with relevant parties about the risk management process been undertaken?
<--- Score

29. What other jobs or tasks affect the performance of the steps in the Supplier Quality Management process?
<--- Score

30. How does your organization track the key measures of product, service, and process quality?
<--- Score

31. How was the detailed process map generated, verified, and validated?
<--- Score

32. What is the cost of poor quality as supported by the team's analysis?
<--- Score

33. Is there a physical segregation of nonconforming material during subsequent storage & processing?
<--- Score

34. Have relevant personnel been informed of outcomes resulting from the consultation process?
<--- Score

35. What are the processes for audit reporting and management?
<--- Score

36. Are in process and final inspections performed where necessary?
<--- Score

37. What did the team gain from developing a sub-process map?
<--- Score

38. Where is the data coming from to measure compliance?
<--- Score

39. Is inspection and test data maintained on file and traceable to each lot?

<--- Score

40. What Supplier Quality Management data should be managed?
<--- Score

41. What type of comparison rate data is available to hiring managers when creating a requisition?
<--- Score

42. Have any additional benefits been identified that will result from closing all or most of the gaps?
<--- Score

43. Who qualifies as a Diverse Supplier for inclusion in the database?
<--- Score

44. Were Pareto charts (or similar) used to portray the 'heavy hitters' (or key sources of variation)?
<--- Score

45. What Supplier Quality Management data should be collected?
<--- Score

46. Where is the process for problem solving defined?
<--- Score

47. Is the Supplier Quality Management process severely broken such that a re-design is necessary?
<--- Score

48. Was a detailed process map created to amplify critical steps of the 'as is' stakeholder process?

<--- Score

49. Are there mechanisms in place to evaluate risk management process?
<--- Score

50. What qualifications and skills do you need?
<--- Score

51. Are kpis defined for all processes?
<--- Score

52. How will the data be checked for quality?
<--- Score

53. What Supplier Quality Management data will be collected?
<--- Score

54. Have tenders been invited from pre-qualified parties?
<--- Score

55. Can the supplier show that corrective actions are applied to other similar processes and products?
<--- Score

56. What data is sent from the application code to the database server?
<--- Score

57. How is data used for program management and improvement?
<--- Score

58. What is your new process flow now that the solution is in place?
<--- Score

59. Did any additional data need to be collected?
<--- Score

60. Is the personnel selected and qualified based on proper education, training and/ or experience?
<--- Score

61. Has the scope for the risk management process been determined?
<--- Score

62. Are records kept to provide evidence that the realization processes and resulting product meets the requirements?
<--- Score

63. Is there any way to speed up the process?
<--- Score

64. How are outputs preserved and protected?
<--- Score

65. Have relevant parties been invited to assist in the risk identification process?
<--- Score

66. What are the stages in the design and development process?
<--- Score

67. Have the processes of your organization been identified?

<--- Score

68. How will corresponding data be collected?
<--- Score

69. Who owns what data?
<--- Score

70. What are the qualifications for suppliers for a specific business classification?
<--- Score

71. Which manufacturing processes are included/ excluded?
<--- Score

72. Do design and development outputs meet requirements of inputs?
<--- Score

73. What is the IT disaster recovery process?
<--- Score

74. What critical process technologies are covered?
<--- Score

75. What are the opportunities for improvement in your supplier quality system?
<--- Score

76. Is the performance gap determined?
<--- Score

77. What tools were used to narrow the list of possible causes?
<--- Score

78. Do you have a documented procedure in place for document and data control?
<--- Score

79. How engaged were you in the implementation process?
<--- Score

80. What were the crucial 'moments of truth' on the process map?
<--- Score

81. How are risks and opportunities addressed?
<--- Score

82. Have the problem and goal statements been updated to reflect the additional knowledge gained from the analyze phase?
<--- Score

83. Do quality systems drive continuous improvement?
<--- Score

84. Are processes needed for the quality management system and application established and maintained?
<--- Score

85. Are additional process changes required to manage the hybrid/eQMS boundary?
<--- Score

86. Is the final output clearly identified?
<--- Score

87. What are the Supplier Quality Management design outputs?
<--- Score

88. Record-keeping requirements flow from the records needed as inputs, outputs, controls and for transformation of a Supplier Quality Management process, are the records needed as inputs to the Supplier Quality Management process available?
<--- Score

89. How secure is the distribution process?
<--- Score

90. Do you show where invoicing data is located?
<--- Score

91. Should you be certifying products or processes?
<--- Score

92. Do purchase orders contain data clearly describing the product or service ordered?
<--- Score

93. Are all team members qualified for all tasks?
<--- Score

94. Are all lots of product identified and traceable through receiving, processing, stock and delivery?
<--- Score

95. What types of data and information does your organization collect?
<--- Score

96. How do you ensure that the Supplier Quality Management opportunity is realistic?
<--- Score

97. Is the design output verified to determine if the input requirements are met?
<--- Score

98. How can risk management be tied procedurally to process elements?
<--- Score

99. What conclusions were drawn from the team's data collection and analysis? How did the team reach these conclusions?
<--- Score

100. How do you get access to the registered data regarding faults of quality?
<--- Score

101. How do you use Supplier Quality Management data and information to support organizational decision making and innovation?
<--- Score

102. What does the data say about the performance of the stakeholder process?
<--- Score

103. When should a process be art not science?
<--- Score

104. Were any designed experiments used to generate additional insight into the data analysis?

<--- Score

105. Are there work instructions for all production processes that affect quality and delivery?
<--- Score

106. Did any value-added analysis or 'lean thinking' take place to identify some of the gaps shown on the 'as is' process map?
<--- Score

107. Are there documented results to evaluate the effectiveness of processes?
<--- Score

108. What is the best way to drive supplier quality management systems?
<--- Score

109. What can be done to improve the training content and process?
<--- Score

110. How do you reduce supplier risk and what is the role of quality in that process?
<--- Score

111. Does the partner have identifiable systems, processes and procedures to support the collaboration?
<--- Score

112. Does the supplier have a tooling database to track and manage tooling?
<--- Score

113. Did you conduct meetings with the supplier to consider quality processes that should be conducted?
<--- Score

114. Is the gap/opportunity displayed and communicated in financial terms?
<--- Score

115. Who will facilitate the team and process?
<--- Score

116. What were the financial benefits resulting from any 'ground fruit or low-hanging fruit' (quick fixes)?
<--- Score

117. Are required inputs and expected outputs identified and documented?
<--- Score

118. How is the design process controlled?
<--- Score

119. What Supplier Quality Management metrics are outputs of the process?
<--- Score

120. Are responsibilities and authorities defined for the design and development process?
<--- Score

121. What quality tools were used to get through the analyze phase?
<--- Score

122. Where are the processes needed for product

realization identified?
<--- Score

123. Have communication processes been established to ensure adequate information flow?
<--- Score

124. What are the revised rough estimates of the financial savings/opportunity for Supplier Quality Management improvements?
<--- Score

125. How do you make sure invoicing data is correct and immediately available to the client?
<--- Score

126. What tools were used to generate the list of possible causes?
<--- Score

127. Are there documented procedures for inspection and testing of product for receiving, in process and final acceptance?
<--- Score

128. Have personnel for assigned duties been qualified by education, training or experience as required?
<--- Score

129. Do you positively identify all products throughout all processing stages?
<--- Score

130. Are design output parameters, including crucial product characteristics, adequately defined

and documented?
<--- Score

131. Does the supplier assure that the data rights provisions are consistent with the subcontract?
<--- Score

Add up total points for this section:
_____ = Total points for this section

Divided by: ______ (number of statements answered) = ______ Average score for this section

Transfer your score to the Supplier Quality Management Index at the beginning of the Self-Assessment.

CRITERION #5: IMPROVE:

INTENT: Develop a practical solution. Innovate, establish and test the solution and to measure the results.

In my belief, the answer to this question is clearly defined:

5 Strongly Agree

4 Agree

3 Neutral

2 Disagree

1 Strongly Disagree

1. How is continuous improvement applied to risk management?
<--- Score

2. Have documented internal audit procedure?
<--- Score

3. Do you require, document and obtain corrective action from your suppliers for nonconforming

materials, parts or services or unsatisfactory performance?
<--- Score

4. Are persons conducting evaluations free from the control of the product developers?
<--- Score

5. Do you show a documented procedure that defines the controls needed for each?
<--- Score

6. Are the results of inspection and testing adequately documented and maintained?
<--- Score

7. What is the team's contingency plan for potential problems occurring in implementation?
<--- Score

8. Are procedures for corrective action documented?
<--- Score

9. Have applicable risks been researched?
<--- Score

10. What were the underlying assumptions on the cost-benefit analysis?
<--- Score

11. Is management reviewing the results?
<--- Score

12. Are new and improved process ('should be') maps developed?

<--- Score

13. Do you currently use any Quality Improvement Tools?
<--- Score

14. Is the implementation plan designed?
<--- Score

15. What importance does your organization management place on developing a quality culture?
<--- Score

16. Have procedures been developed and implemented to identify existing and potential quality issues?
<--- Score

17. What tools were used to evaluate the potential solutions?
<--- Score

18. Are organization policies, objectives, and its commitment to quality documented?
<--- Score

19. How do textile companies mitigate supply chain risks?
<--- Score

20. Does it offer guidance on the decisions that leaders in creativity-dependent businesses have to make?
<--- Score

21. Are training needs identified and documented?
<--- Score

22. What lessons, if any, from a pilot were incorporated into the design of the full-scale solution?
<--- Score

23. What tools were used to tap into the creativity and encourage 'outside the box' thinking?
<--- Score

24. Are the key business and technology risks being managed?
<--- Score

25. What error proofing will be done to address some of the discrepancies observed in the 'as is' process?
<--- Score

26. Is there a small-scale pilot for proposed improvement(s)? What conclusions were drawn from the outcomes of a pilot?
<--- Score

27. Has your organization developed its emergency response, continuity and recovery strategies?
<--- Score

28. How does your organization justify expenditures on quality improvements?
<--- Score

29. Are needs & expectations from interested parties identified and documented?
<--- Score

30. How is knowledge sharing about risk management improved?
<--- Score

31. What attendant changes will need to be made to ensure that the solution is successful?
<--- Score

32. Who do you report Supplier Quality Management results to?
<--- Score

33. What are the unmet needs of organizations that suppliers can develop capabilities for?
<--- Score

34. Are metrics used to evaluate and manage Vendors?
<--- Score

35. What alternative responses are available to manage risk?
<--- Score

36. Has your organization identified a need for improvements to the quality management system?
<--- Score

37. How did the team generate the list of possible solutions?
<--- Score

38. Are the most efficient solutions problem-specific?
<--- Score

39. Are procedures documented for managing Supplier Quality Management risks?
<--- Score

40. Are any audit findings properly documented and is there evidence of actions taken?
<--- Score

41. Do you demonstrate that Suppliers QMS effectiveness continually improves?
<--- Score

42. To what extent does management recognize Supplier Quality Management as a tool to increase the results?
<--- Score

43. Where is product design input requirements documented?
<--- Score

44. Are the policies understood, implemented, and maintained at all levels of your organization?
<--- Score

45. How does the solution remove the key sources of issues discovered in the analyze phase?
<--- Score

46. Who manages supplier risk management in your organization?
<--- Score

47. Do you systematically give feedback to improve the quality, effectiveness, value and

service that your suppliers provide?
<--- Score

48. Does the solution enable increased integration with external suppliers or users?
<--- Score

49. Is the optimal solution selected based on testing and analysis?
<--- Score

50. Does vendor have a documented corrective action program in place?
<--- Score

51. Have the most appropriate options for treating risks been determined and selected?
<--- Score

52. How important are issues when selecting and evaluating preferred suppliers?
<--- Score

53. Have approved and authorized distribution channels been clearly documented?
<--- Score

54. Have specific improvement projects been identified?
<--- Score

55. Does vendor have a documented complaint policy and procedures in place?
<--- Score

56. What are the evaluation criteria?

<--- Score

57. Were any criteria developed to assist the team in testing and evaluating potential solutions?
<--- Score

58. Can achieve its intended results?
<--- Score

59. Is documented information maintained as the result of management reviews?
<--- Score

60. Would you develop a Supplier Quality Management Communication Strategy?
<--- Score

61. Are procedures of performing internal quality audits documented?
<--- Score

62. Have critical success factors, goals or objectives for the area included in scope been documented?
<--- Score

63. Do you understand all the requirements?
<--- Score

64. Is there a cost/benefit analysis of optimal solution(s)?
<--- Score

65. Does your organization have a documented quality manual?
<--- Score

66. Are design changes appropriately reviewed, controlled, and documented?
<--- Score

67. How do you measure risk?
<--- Score

68. Does higher quality result in increased sales?
<--- Score

69. Are the results of internal audits communicated to top management?
<--- Score

70. What is Supplier Quality Management risk?
<--- Score

71. Are documented information maintained as evidence of conformity with the acceptance criteria?
<--- Score

72. What is the implementation plan?
<--- Score

73. Does the supplier have a documented program to perform internal audits of the quality system?
<--- Score

74. What risks do you need to manage?
<--- Score

75. Do you evaluate and select suppliers based on the ability to meet your quality requirements?
<--- Score

76. Are all associated contractual terms, conditions, quality clauses and customer specifications reviewed, approved and documented?
<--- Score

77. Do you determine and implement actions taken during as a result of nonconformance?
<--- Score

78. Is the Supplier Quality Management documentation thorough?
<--- Score

79. Was a pilot designed for the proposed solution(s)?
<--- Score

80. What communications are necessary to support the implementation of the solution?
<--- Score

81. Is Supplier Quality Management documentation maintained?
<--- Score

82. Are possible solutions generated and tested?
<--- Score

83. How is the QMS continually improved?
<--- Score

84. Are procedures for handling, storage, packaging, and delivery developed, documented and maintained?
<--- Score

85. Does your solution offer any type of chat functionality, similar to popular consumer tools?
<--- Score

86. What is managements role in the development of a quality system?
<--- Score

87. Describe the design of the pilot and what tests were conducted, if any?
<--- Score

88. Are improved process ('should be') maps modified based on pilot data and analysis?
<--- Score

89. Has your organization identified and documented its interested parties relevant to the QMS?
<--- Score

90. How would implementing ISO 9000 improve the way your organization does business?
<--- Score

91. Does the supplier maintain up to date quality records used to evaluate sub-suppliers performance?
<--- Score

92. How does the workforce support and improve its workforce capability and capacity?
<--- Score

93. Have documented preventive action

procedure?
<--- Score

94. How is the effectiveness of the WHS system evaluated?
<--- Score

95. Can the solution be designed and implemented within an acceptable time period?
<--- Score

96. What tools were most useful during the improve phase?
<--- Score

97. Are the best solutions selected?
<--- Score

98. Does your organization foster an environment that emphasizes continual improvement?
<--- Score

99. What should a proof of concept or pilot accomplish?
<--- Score

100. Is a quality policy defined, documented, understood, implemented, and maintained?
<--- Score

101. Why perform a risk assessment of suppliers?
<--- Score

102. Does your organization use corrective and preventive actions for continual improvement purposes?

<--- Score

103. Do staff members understand the Quality Policy?
<--- Score

104. How do you measure improved Supplier Quality Management service perception, and satisfaction?
<--- Score

105. Are there any constraints (technical, political, cultural, or otherwise) that would inhibit certain solutions?
<--- Score

106. Have the quality system compliance requirements for the relevant work activity been documented?
<--- Score

107. How will the group know that the solution worked?
<--- Score

108. How are design and development changes identified?
<--- Score

109. For estimation problems, how do you develop an estimation statement?
<--- Score

110. Are internal audits documented and kept on file?
<--- Score

111. Are risk management tasks balanced centrally and locally?
<--- Score

112. How can skill-level changes improve Supplier Quality Management?
<--- Score

113. Are criteria for selection and periodic evaluation of suppliers defined?
<--- Score

114. Does vendor have a documented quality policy?
<--- Score

115. Are documented information maintained for the design and development activities?
<--- Score

116. Has your organization identified and documented potential changes?
<--- Score

117. What is Supplier Quality Management's impact on utilizing the best solution(s)?
<--- Score

118. Has the scope management document been updated and distributed to help prevent scope creep?
<--- Score

119. Are measures used to evaluate overall quality?
<--- Score

120. Where do you start your risk journey?
<--- Score

121. How will the team or the process owner(s) monitor the implementation plan to see that it is working as intended?
<--- Score

122. Does your organization provide customer feedback for future improvement?
<--- Score

123. What criteria will you use to assess your Supplier Quality Management risks?
<--- Score

124. What is the benefit of understanding the value adding from the supply chain perspective?
<--- Score

125. Is the scope clearly documented?
<--- Score

126. Does your organization have a defined and documented quality policy and quality objectives?
<--- Score

127. How is organizational knowledge documented and shared?
<--- Score

128. What does the 'should be' process map/design look like?
<--- Score

129. Does your organization determined the nature, duration and complexity of design and development?
<--- Score

130. How can organization appropriate quality procedures be developed?
<--- Score

131. Are documented information on results of changes and any necessary actions maintained?
<--- Score

132. How can team cohesiveness be developed?
<--- Score

133. Are the risks fully understood, reasonable and manageable?
<--- Score

134. Is there any other Supplier Quality Management solution?
<--- Score

135. Are the required measurements identified and documented?
<--- Score

136. Is there a documented procedure controlling internal audits?
<--- Score

137. Are the results of actions taken recorded?
<--- Score

138. How will you measure the results?

<--- Score

139. What are the Supplier Quality Management security risks?
<--- Score

140. Does management support the identification and resolution of potential nonconformities to prevent occurrence?
<--- Score

141. Is pilot data collected and analyzed?
<--- Score

142. How /where are design and development responsibilities and authorities defined?
<--- Score

143. Are inspection instructions and results properly documented?
<--- Score

144. Are there documented procedures to control customer and industry drawings and specifications?
<--- Score

145. Does the system have established procedures for managing hazards and risks?
<--- Score

146. Can you integrate quality management and risk management?
<--- Score

147. Is the quality policy documented or / and

posted within your organization?
<--- Score

148. Are your organization Quality Goals & Objectives documented?
<--- Score

149. What other types of supply chain risks are common?
<--- Score

150. Are the audit results recorded and brought to the attention of the responsible personnel?
<--- Score

151. Do the viable solutions scale to future needs?
<--- Score

152. Are audit results documented and reviewed by management?
<--- Score

153. Have parts and supplier quality been documented for parts selection?
<--- Score

154. What improvement actions were done and what efficiency obtained?
<--- Score

155. What assumptions are made about the solution and approach?
<--- Score

156. Are documented information maintained as evidence of management reviews?

<--- Score

157. Is the Supplier Quality Management solution sustainable?
<--- Score

158. Have documented corrective action procedure?
<--- Score

159. Do representatives of all functions concerned identify, document, review, and approve all design changes before the change is implemented?
<--- Score

160. Are suppliers evaluated to assure that material supplied meets customer requirements?
<--- Score

161. Who are the Supplier Quality Management decision-makers?
<--- Score

162. Is a solution implementation plan established, including schedule/work breakdown structure, resources, risk management plan, cost/budget, and control plan?
<--- Score

163. Is there a documented procedure defining the requirements for reviewing nonconformities?
<--- Score

164. Who are the Supplier Quality Management decision makers?
<--- Score

165. Do you document the results of all inspection and testing?
<--- Score

166. Is there a documented training program?
<--- Score

167. Are results to be achieve are clearly defined?
<--- Score

168. Is there a procedure for the receipt and evaluation of customer complaints?
<--- Score

169. Is a contingency plan established?
<--- Score

Add up total points for this section:
_____ = Total points for this section

Divided by: ______ (number of statements answered) = ______ Average score for this section

Transfer your score to the Supplier Quality Management Index at the beginning of the Self-Assessment.

CRITERION #6: CONTROL:

INTENT: Implement the practical solution. Maintain the performance and correct possible complications.

In my belief, the answer to this question is clearly defined:

5 Strongly Agree

4 Agree

3 Neutral

2 Disagree

1 Strongly Disagree

1. How are the information and control systems used?
<--- Score

2. How are production and service provision changes controlled?
<--- Score

3. Does job training on the documented procedures

need to be part of the process team's education and training?
<--- Score

4. What other areas of the group might benefit from the Supplier Quality Management team's improvements, knowledge, and learning?
<--- Score

5. How are products and services manufactured and/or provided under controlled conditions?
<--- Score

6. Is new knowledge gained imbedded in the response plan?
<--- Score

7. How do you plan for the cost of succession?
<--- Score

8. Is there a routine maintenance or service contract in place for the climate control system?
<--- Score

9. Do you periodically review supplier performance and use corresponding reviews as a basis for establishing the level of controls to be implemented?
<--- Score

10. What controls are in place to manage and monitor production processes?
<--- Score

11. How are operational processes planned and controlled?

<--- Score

12. Act/Adjust: What Do you Need to Do Differently?
<--- Score

13. How do you determine the type and extent of control applied to the supplier and the purchased product?
<--- Score

14. Are project progress reports and costs regularly reviewed and compared with base line plans?
<--- Score

15. Do outputs include or reference monitoring and measuring methods, and acceptance criteria, as applicable?
<--- Score

16. What are the known security controls?
<--- Score

17. Are the Supplier Quality Management standards challenging?
<--- Score

18. Are quality objectives monitored and reviewed at reasonable intervals?
<--- Score

19. Do you evaluate the effectiveness of change processes against agreed objectives?
<--- Score

20. Is there planning to monitor and review

Quality Objectives at reasonable intervals?
<--- Score

21. Has the improved process and its steps been standardized?
<--- Score

22. Are the component & supplier quality plans been reviewed and updated?
<--- Score

23. What are barriers facing your organization to start implement ISO 9000 standards?
<--- Score

24. Are operating procedures consistent?
<--- Score

25. How will the day-to-day responsibilities for monitoring and continual improvement be transferred from the improvement team to the process owner?
<--- Score

26. Are processes that cannot be verified after production monitored and controlled throughout the processes?
<--- Score

27. Are all items of equipment and instruments controlled, calibrated, and maintained?
<--- Score

28. Have all monitoring and measuring activities determined?
<--- Score

29. Are there documented procedures?
<--- Score

30. Are responsibilities defined in design activity plans?
<--- Score

31. What are the outputs of product realization planning?
<--- Score

32. What are the calibration standards used for each type of equipment?
<--- Score

33. Is a response plan established and deployed?
<--- Score

34. How will Supplier Quality Management decisions be made and monitored?
<--- Score

35. How will the process owner and team be able to hold the gains?
<--- Score

36. Is the business continuity plan established?
<--- Score

37. Can you adapt and adjust to changing Supplier Quality Management situations?
<--- Score

38. Is a documented training plan established that identified operator basic training needs?

<--- Score

39. Are monitoring and measuring resources Suitability maintained?
<--- Score

40. How will new or emerging customer needs/ requirements be checked/communicated to orient the process toward meeting the new specifications and continually reducing variation?
<--- Score

41. Is there a recommended audit plan for routine surveillance inspections of Supplier Quality Management's gains?
<--- Score

42. Implementation Planning: is a pilot needed to test the changes before a full roll out occurs?
<--- Score

43. Does the Supplier Quality Management performance meet the customer's requirements?
<--- Score

44. Are subcontract requirements flowed down into appropriate program plans and implementing procedures?
<--- Score

45. Are important routine maintenance procedures for the climate control system conducted?
<--- Score

46. Do design projects receive adequate planning?

<--- Score

47. Are new process steps, standards, and documentation ingrained into normal operations?
<--- Score

48. How are monitoring and measuring resources controlled?
<--- Score

49. Will any special training be provided for results interpretation?
<--- Score

50. Is there a transfer of ownership and knowledge to process owner and process team tasked with the responsibilities.
<--- Score

51. How does your organization benchmark itself against other companies?
<--- Score

52. Has your organization defined a plan or strategy to meet the Quality Goals and Objectives?
<--- Score

53. Are suggested corrective/restorative actions indicated on the response plan for known causes to problems that might surface?
<--- Score

54. Is knowledge gained on process shared and institutionalized?
<--- Score

55. Does the plan exist and is controlled?
<--- Score

56. How do your controls stack up?
<--- Score

57. Are planned arrangements in place to ensure achievement of the product and service requirements?
<--- Score

58. Which business plan format is right for you?
<--- Score

59. Is there documentation that will support the successful operation of the improvement?
<--- Score

60. Who is the Supplier Quality Management process owner?
<--- Score

61. Has your organization implemented a system to monitor its tooling management activities if any worked is outsourced?
<--- Score

62. Has the supplier determined when the plan will be implemented?
<--- Score

63. Does your organization have a Quality Control Manual?
<--- Score

64. What quality tools were useful in the control

phase?
<--- Score

65. Has the supplier determined when will the plan be implemented?
<--- Score

66. Have all the specified technical requirements/ standards specified been fully understood?
<--- Score

67. Does the supplier have a system to manage and track all sub-tier advance planning activity?
<--- Score

68. What is the process for monitoring and review of the external and internal issues?
<--- Score

69. What are the critical parameters to watch?
<--- Score

70. What is the recommended frequency of auditing?
<--- Score

71. Are documented procedures clear and easy to follow for the operators?
<--- Score

72. Are design input requirements reviewed for adequacy with applicable standards, regulations, and statutory requirements?
<--- Score

73. What barriers facing your organization to start implement ISO 9000 standards?

<--- Score

74. Are production and service operations carried out under controlled conditions?
<--- Score

75. What adjustments to the strategies are needed?
<--- Score

76. Are parts and supplier quality being monitored for modifications?
<--- Score

77. Are there procedures for identifying and planning for processes that directly affect quality?
<--- Score

78. Who is responsible for implementing the response / control?
<--- Score

79. What other systems, operations, processes, and infrastructures (hiring practices, staffing, training, incentives/rewards, metrics/dashboards/scorecards, etc.) need updates, additions, changes, or deletions in order to facilitate knowledge transfer and improvements?
<--- Score

80. Are parts and supplier quality being monitored?
<--- Score

81. How will the process owner verify improvement in present and future sigma levels, process capabilities?
<--- Score

82. Is the product uniquely identified in relation to any required traceability to specifications or standards?
<--- Score

83. Does the response plan contain a definite closed loop continual improvement scheme (e.g., plan-do-check-act)?
<--- Score

84. Has the project plan been reviewed by personnel involved or affected by the project?
<--- Score

85. Are criteria and methods monitored, measured, and reviewed through performance indicators?
<--- Score

86. Does the supplier software Quality program include a supplier control system that includes?
<--- Score

87. Which roles are planning to use IIoT to monitor and improve quality?
<--- Score

88. Are any deviations from plans identified and actions taken to meet the original project program?
<--- Score

89. How might the group capture best practices and lessons learned so as to leverage improvements?
<--- Score

90. Does the laboratory operate under a unique quality assurance project plan?
<--- Score

91. How does your organization develop and implement plans and strategies for the short term?
<--- Score

92. Is there a control plan in place for sustaining improvements (short and long-term)?
<--- Score

93. Are activities for verification defined in the Design Plan?
<--- Score

94. What is the control/monitoring plan?
<--- Score

95. Are controls in place and consistently applied?
<--- Score

96. How is the release of product and services controlled?
<--- Score

97. Is a response plan in place for when the input, process, or output measures indicate an 'out-of-control' condition?
<--- Score

98. Are production processes defined, planned, and documented?
<--- Score

99. How are information and control systems used?
<--- Score

100. How is customer satisfaction monitored?
<--- Score

101. How do you monitor supplier performance?
<--- Score

102. What is the overall IT security control plan?
<--- Score

103. Are processes, procedures, records and customer complaints reviewed and analyzed in order to improve your standards of quality?
<--- Score

104. What is effective supplier performance monitoring?
<--- Score

105. Does Supplier Quality Management appropriately measure and monitor risk?
<--- Score

106. Does the supplier have a quality plan in place, and is it reviewed on a regular basis?
<--- Score

107. Have new or revised work instructions resulted?
<--- Score

108. Does the resource management plan include a personnel development plan?
<--- Score

109. Are plans drawn up to identify the responsibility of each design and development activity?
<--- Score

110. Does your organization determine what needs to be monitored and measured?
<--- Score

111. What should the next improvement project be that is related to Supplier Quality Management?
<--- Score

112. What are your future plans for expansion, if any?
<--- Score

113. Is the supplier required to generate a documented software Quality program plan with instructions?
<--- Score

114. Does a troubleshooting guide exist or is it needed?
<--- Score

115. Is reporting being used or needed?
<--- Score

116. Have you implemented initiatives to your support workforce planning objectives?
<--- Score

117. Are there mechanisms in place to implement and monitor the action plan?

<--- Score

118. How is property owned by customers or external providers controlled?
<--- Score

119. What key inputs and outputs are being measured on an ongoing basis?
<--- Score

120. Is there a standardized process?
<--- Score

121. Is there a documented and implemented monitoring plan?
<--- Score

122. Does the supplier assure that all software plans required by the subcontract are?
<--- Score

123. Are activities for Validation defined and performed per the plan and documented?
<--- Score

124. Does the laboratory operate under a quality management plan?
<--- Score

125. How do you promote supplier monitoring of the performance of manufacturing processes?
<--- Score

126. How will input, process, and output variables be checked to detect for sub-optimal conditions?
<--- Score

127. How well what quality and standards apply?
<--- Score

128. Does your organization apply suitable methods for monitoring, and where applicable, measurement of the QMS?
<--- Score

129. Are authorities and responsibilities for prompt, effective resolution of quality related issues and quality planning clearly defined?
<--- Score

130. What roles and responsibilities can quality management groups have at a large manufacturing plant?
<--- Score

131. Are plans reviewed and updated as the design evolves?
<--- Score

132. Why monitor and manage suppliers performance?
<--- Score

133. How will report readings be checked to effectively monitor performance?
<--- Score

134. Is the design & development transfer stage planned?
<--- Score

Add up total points for this section:

_____ = Total points for this section

Divided by: ______ (number of statements answered) = ______ Average score for this section

Transfer your score to the Supplier Quality Management Index at the beginning of the Self-Assessment.

CRITERION #7: SUSTAIN:

INTENT: Retain the benefits.

In my belief, the answer to this question is clearly defined:

5 Strongly Agree

4 Agree

3 Neutral

2 Disagree

1 Strongly Disagree

1. Where and how will the training be delivered?
<--- Score

2. What is dynamic management of supplier?
<--- Score

3. Are resource available to implement the change?
<--- Score

4. Do you have access to the executive team?

<--- Score

5. How are qms awareness and relevant information communicated?
<--- Score

6. What is the level of detail for the procedure contents?
<--- Score

7. What are the performance metrics and targets for Discovery Sessions?
<--- Score

8. Are action items captured and managed?
<--- Score

9. What are the boundaries of an audit?
<--- Score

10. Is there a dedicated, reliable support team available for your program?
<--- Score

11. Is the design effectively communicated?
<--- Score

12. What type of search capability is available to hiring managers?
<--- Score

13. What is a quality management system?
<--- Score

14. What are the reasons for having a purchasing quality group?

<--- Score

15. Do you justify the approach from a compliance perspective?
<--- Score

16. Where does supplier quality function fit in the management of internal suppliers?
<--- Score

17. How does your organization achieve customer engagement?
<--- Score

18. What new services of functionality will be implemented next with Supplier Quality Management ?
<--- Score

19. How well does your organization listen to the voice of the customer?
<--- Score

20. Who is on the team?
<--- Score

21. Has a management representative been appointed?
<--- Score

22. Are referee contact details correct?
<--- Score

23. What is the overall business strategy?
<--- Score

24. What is the suppliers quality management policy?
<--- Score

25. Has a quality manual been prepared?
<--- Score

26. Which topics are covered in the training programs?
<--- Score

27. How are Six Sigma projects selected?
<--- Score

28. Is evidence of compliance available?
<--- Score

29. Do you have a good quality manager?
<--- Score

30. Do you still have a relationship with your salesperson?
<--- Score

31. Can you do all this work?
<--- Score

32. Are quality objectives communicated in any sort of media/form?
<--- Score

33. Which procedures or guidelines are used as part of your quality system?
<--- Score

34. Have benefits been optimized with all key

stakeholders?
<--- Score

35. How is management review conducted?
<--- Score

36. How is the location and status of assets and material tracked?
<--- Score

37. What type of changes must be done by the VMS provider?
<--- Score

38. Does each group have a different perspective and expectation of what constitutes quality?
<--- Score

39. How is customer communication handled?
<--- Score

40. Are production records adequately prepared and maintained?
<--- Score

41. Can the system handle monthly timesheets?
<--- Score

42. Why not do Supplier Quality Management?
<--- Score

43. Are all delivery terms listed on purchase order correct and acceptable?
<--- Score

44. Do you think Supplier Quality Management

accomplishes the goals you expect it to accomplish?
<--- Score

45. Is the method for obtaining and using the customer satisfaction information determined?
<--- Score

46. Have all deliverables been according to SLA and quality levels?
<--- Score

47. How are supplier relationships studied?
<--- Score

48. Do you currently have a method for measuring supplier performance criteria?
<--- Score

49. Do you provide supplier support and training?
<--- Score

50. Are you listed on project procurement sites?
<--- Score

51. Where in the QMS should Quality Metrics be established?
<--- Score

52. How are resources determined and allocated?
<--- Score

53. How is your organization structured?
<--- Score

54. Why only service after breakdowns?
<--- Score

55. What is your top goal in managing your suppliers?
<--- Score

56. Are total quality management programs a fact or a management fad?
<--- Score

57. Has a person been assigned the responsibility of administering the quality system?
<--- Score

58. What is the level of detail for the report contents?
<--- Score

59. What type of equipment or people tenders the service?
<--- Score

60. Who will coordinate your organizations emergency response, continuity and recovery strategies?
<--- Score

61. Are management procedures in place and available to all employees effecting quality?
<--- Score

62. Is lost, damaged, or unsuitable product reported to the customer?
<--- Score

63. Why become a certified supply quality professional?

<--- Score

64. Is the impact that Supplier Quality Management has shown?
<--- Score

65. Has an ISO 9000 management representative been appointed?
<--- Score

66. What happens to a production line if a supplier or a suppliers supplier cannot deliver quality goods on-time?
<--- Score

67. Who are four people whose careers you have enhanced?
<--- Score

68. How do you assist with time entry to ensure hours are categorized properly?
<--- Score

69. What advantages and disadvantages exist for your organization in becoming ISO certified?
<--- Score

70. Is there evidence that the product was inspected and tested?
<--- Score

71. Who else should you help?
<--- Score

72. What are the top 3 things at the forefront of your Supplier Quality Management agendas for the next 3

years?
<--- Score

73. Where do you host the system and what level of security is provided at the center?
<--- Score

74. How efficiently must you use your remaining resources?
<--- Score

75. Which of most closely represents the view of different groups in your organization?
<--- Score

76. What steps are taken to tamper proof products?
<--- Score

77. What is quality and quality management?
<--- Score

78. What type of employee background checks are conducted and how frequently?
<--- Score

79. How to initiate collaboration from the lean supply chain context?
<--- Score

80. What may be the consequences for the performance of an organization if all stakeholders are not consulted regarding Supplier Quality Management?
<--- Score

81. Are all members of the quality staff independent of production responsibilities?
<--- Score

82. Are effectiveness of any corrective actions taken verified?
<--- Score

83. Do supplier quality records include at a minimum?
<--- Score

84. What is the quality of the product?
<--- Score

85. What is the value to your organization?
<--- Score

86. Will service follow manufacturing into decline?
<--- Score

87. Is your organization societally responsible?
<--- Score

88. Ask yourself: how would you do this work if you only had one staff member to do it?
<--- Score

89. Can supplier quality management be completely outsourced to the supplier?
<--- Score

90. Are all samples handled to avoid contamination and/or loss of material during field operation?
<--- Score

91. How to create the structured supply chain responsiveness?
<--- Score

92. Why supplier quality is critical?
<--- Score

93. How do you create buy-in?
<--- Score

94. How is configuration management performed?
<--- Score

95. What objectives has your organization set?
<--- Score

96. In a project to restructure Supplier Quality Management outcomes, which stakeholders would you involve?
<--- Score

97. What is your organization Collaboration?
<--- Score

98. Have you completed the project correctly?
<--- Score

99. How are internal audits managed?
<--- Score

100. How does your organization capture the voice of the customer?
<--- Score

101. How are staff encouraged to implement a

quality system?
<--- Score

102. Is your quality policy communicated throughout your organization and review for continuing suitability?
<--- Score

103. What are the best practices to facilitate the efficient implementation of a QMS based on ISO 15189?
<--- Score

104. Why performance management for suppliers?
<--- Score

105. What kind of defect in quality do you register?
<--- Score

106. Do you have access to system audit trails?
<--- Score

107. Are individual training records easily accessible to each employee?
<--- Score

108. Is your quality program certified?
<--- Score

109. Are the records from the management review maintained?
<--- Score

110. Do you share critical information with partners and suppliers for mutual benefit?

<--- Score

111. How does Six Sigma bring about a reduction of defects?
<--- Score

112. Are all agreements with clients and service providers in place?
<--- Score

113. Do you see more potential in people than they do in themselves?
<--- Score

114. Is there an up to date organization chart?
<--- Score

115. How many levels and/or tiers are typically in your supply chain?
<--- Score

116. How are corrective actions managed?
<--- Score

117. Is the Supplier Quality Management organization completing tasks effectively and efficiently?
<--- Score

118. What formal performance management in place and reported?
<--- Score

119. How is input provided to management review?
<--- Score

120. Is product in stock periodically checked?
<--- Score

121. Are new benefits received and understood?
<--- Score

122. How are new contract workers fed to downstream HRIS tools or identity/asset management tools?
<--- Score

123. What is the effect of respect for individuals within the work area?
<--- Score

124. Is there an established WHS system?
<--- Score

125. How difficult is it to ensure traceability with separate systems?
<--- Score

126. How are customer concerns handled?
<--- Score

127. Why is supplier quality so critical?
<--- Score

128. Are there concerns that might be shared by customers or suppliers?
<--- Score

129. Did you conduct a performance rating of the supplier after execution?
<--- Score

130. Have new benefits been realized?
<--- Score

131. What relationships among Supplier Quality Management trends do you perceive?
<--- Score

132. Is there a management policy and objectives for, and commitment to, quality?
<--- Score

133. What is the background of the management team?
<--- Score

134. How complex is the part to manufacture?
<--- Score

135. What sort of reporting does your organization use?
<--- Score

136. What mechanisms does your organization have in place to receive feedback from customers?
<--- Score

137. What management and quality theories are best for small businesses?
<--- Score

138. Which individuals, teams or departments will be involved in Supplier Quality Management?
<--- Score

139. How are you managing supplier compliance today?

<--- Score

140. How can team success be ensured?
<--- Score

141. What maintenance system is in operation?
<--- Score

142. Are your suppliers obliged to take back materials?
<--- Score

143. Which topics are stressed in employee participation groups?
<--- Score

144. What trophy do you want on your mantle?
<--- Score

145. Why should minority businesses join Corporate Plus?
<--- Score

146. What was the timeline for implementation, from the contract signature to deployment?
<--- Score

147. Are the materials and equipment referred to in the specification available?
<--- Score

148. Are internal system audits performed on a regularly scheduled basis?
<--- Score

149. Why do some organizations struggle to

manage quality?
<--- Score

150. Are reviewed by quality management?
<--- Score

151. What management system can you use to leverage the Supplier Quality Management experience, ideas, and concerns of the people closest to the work to be done?
<--- Score

152. What attributes would you expect to be present in your organization that has a sound quality system?
<--- Score

153. Are personnel involved in design verification provided with the necessary resources?
<--- Score

154. Which of most closely represents the view of the different groups in your organization?
<--- Score

155. Is there a system in place to notify customers of potential non conforming material?
<--- Score

156. What is the future of quality management software?
<--- Score

157. Are all measuring and test equipment used on products, including employee owned inspection equipment, calibrated on a regular basis?

<--- Score

158. What is the future holds for supply chain management?
<--- Score

159. Are all quality tools applicable only to the quality field?
<--- Score

160. Is your basic point ______ or ______?
<--- Score

161. Are records of training maintained?
<--- Score

162. Whom among your colleagues do you trust, and for what?
<--- Score

163. How to juggle individual based pay with team based pay?
<--- Score

164. Does supplier have an internal organization?
<--- Score

165. Is there a supplier corrective action system?
<--- Score

166. What projects are going on in the organization today, and what resources are those projects using from the resource pools?
<--- Score

167. What is your quality managers work?

<--- Score

168. Are corrected nonconforming products and services verified for compliance after rework?
<--- Score

169. What do we do when new problems arise?
<--- Score

170. Is there harm done to the participants?
<--- Score

171. What are the various implications for managers to overcome supply chain challenges?
<--- Score

172. Is your response in a simple format?
<--- Score

173. How many employees go into Quality as a profession?
<--- Score

174. How are changes to the QMS handled?
<--- Score

175. Are records maintained to indicate the person who released conforming product at all pertinent stages?
<--- Score

176. Are you going to perform all of tests in order to sell to a variety of customers?
<--- Score

177. Are delivery dates listed on purchase order

correct and achievable?
<--- Score

178. What do successful competitors do?
<--- Score

179. Has your organization implemented a supplier performance management program?
<--- Score

180. Where are you personally on the ethical chain?
<--- Score

181. Are the suppliers and quality certified?
<--- Score

182. Are your business goals aligned with the prospective collaboration partners strategic goals?
<--- Score

183. Are production machines and equipment appropriate for the product being produced?
<--- Score

184. Are corrective actions taken appropriate to the effects of the nonconformities encountered?
<--- Score

185. Is the material packaged or otherwise modified by your organization?
<--- Score

186. Is the part custom built or off-the-shelf?
<--- Score

187. Are records maintained of management reviews?
<--- Score

188. Is the relative price of a substitute product/ service low compared to existing?
<--- Score

189. How can quality management groups be organized?
<--- Score

190. Do you conduct management reviews meetings in according to an established schedule?
<--- Score

191. Have you determined the competence for personal affecting product quality?
<--- Score

192. What gets examined?
<--- Score

193. How is implementation research currently incorporated into each of your goals?
<--- Score

194. If there were zero limitations, what would you do differently?
<--- Score

195. Are production machines and equipment clean and adequately maintained?
<--- Score

196. Are actions taken appropriate to the effects, or potential effects of the nonconformity?
<--- Score

197. What types of cultures promote exceptional quality management?
<--- Score

198. Are the assumptions believable and achievable?
<--- Score

199. What other tools do you use to ensure supplier quality?
<--- Score

200. Does the partner have aligned management teams?
<--- Score

201. Can the technical and quality managers be the same person?
<--- Score

202. Does the finance and accounting system play roles in the quality management system?
<--- Score

203. Who are the highest-quality suppliers?
<--- Score

204. What level of visibility do you have?
<--- Score

205. How is the communication between your organization and its suppliers managed?
<--- Score

206. Is there an WHS induction and training program and is it made available to all employees?
<--- Score

207. Does the supplier have an effective material management system?
<--- Score

208. What about the vendors culture made it different from the others?
<--- Score

209. Do you implement programs to ensure your workplace is an employer of choice?
<--- Score

210. How do you manage supplier quality?
<--- Score

211. Who is responsible for Supplier Quality Management?
<--- Score

212. What have you done to protect your business from competitive encroachment?
<--- Score

213. How satisfied are the customers?
<--- Score

214. Is it a quality product that will last?
<--- Score

215. Does the supplier have an up-to-date material management system?

<--- Score

216. Why close partnership is so great?
<--- Score

217. Is there a procedure / system as a guideline to conduct customer satisfaction surveys?
<--- Score

218. Does supplier have a quality manual?
<--- Score

219. Are the quality objectives measurable and consistent with the quality policy?
<--- Score

220. Are audits scheduled on the basis of the status and importance of the activity?
<--- Score

221. Why would your organization use simultaneous engineering?
<--- Score

222. What assistance does your organization expect from its partners?
<--- Score

223. What are the core activities you are responsible for?
<--- Score

224. What was the last experiment you ran?
<--- Score

225. What are the business goals Supplier Quality

Management is aiming to achieve?
<--- Score

226. What is your top challenge in bringing new products to market?
<--- Score

227. Is worker satisfaction related to productivity or quality?
<--- Score

228. In retrospect, of the projects that you pulled the plug on, what percent do you wish had been allowed to keep going, and what percent do you wish had ended earlier?
<--- Score

229. How long has your program been in place?
<--- Score

230. How do you become a Quality supplier?
<--- Score

231. Who are the primary customers of your organization?
<--- Score

232. At what moment would you think; Will I get fired?
<--- Score

233. Are there records of the training?
<--- Score

234. Are there established and maintained procedures to training activities?
<--- Score

235. Have you provided all the information requested?
<--- Score

236. Who is the main stakeholder, with ultimate responsibility for driving Supplier Quality Management forward?
<--- Score

237. Is appropriate to your organization?
<--- Score

238. Does the supplier review procedures to assure that software engineering reviews include?
<--- Score

239. Who is responsible assuring compliance?
<--- Score

240. What is the Quality Policy and how is it communicated?
<--- Score

241. Are records of reviews and audits maintained?
<--- Score

242. How configurable is the workflow embedded within the system?
<--- Score

243. What is one way that your organization can show the quality of its respect for individuals?
<--- Score

244. How do you listen to customers to obtain actionable information?
<--- Score

245. How acts the leader in a supply chain?
<--- Score

246. Is nonconforming product adequately segregated?
<--- Score

247. What role does top management play with respect to supplier quality management?
<--- Score

248. How does Supplier Quality Management integrate with other stakeholder initiatives?
<--- Score

249. Will it be accepted by users?
<--- Score

250. Can sustainable quality management contribute to your organizational performance?
<--- Score

251. What is the attitude and involvement of top management?
<--- Score

252. Does the supply chain have sufficient spare capacity to undertake the work?
<--- Score

253. Can employers build consensus around foundational quality management principles for

talent suppliers?
<--- Score

254. What are the strengths of your supplier quality system?
<--- Score

255. Why be concerned with supplier quality?
<--- Score

256. Does the whs system include participative arrangements?
<--- Score

257. Do you use a multidisciplinary approach to prepare for product realization?
<--- Score

258. Who is responsible for measuring supplier performance?
<--- Score

259. Have you demonstrated your ability to meet all of the selection criteria?
<--- Score

260. Where can information be obtained?
<--- Score

261. Why is it important to treat ones own employees as the most important customers?
<--- Score

262. What is the source of the strategies for Supplier Quality Management strengthening and reform?
<--- Score

263. What is your organizations industry?
<--- Score

264. How much information do the hiring managers have to provide in order to create a requisition?
<--- Score

265. What kind of culture does your organization want?
<--- Score

266. What is the criticality of the part?
<--- Score

267. Does top management assure that quality objectives are measurable and consistent with the quality policy?
<--- Score

268. If you were responsible for initiating and implementing major changes in your organization, what steps might you take to ensure acceptance of those changes?
<--- Score

269. Do you use supplier quality surveillance to try to ensure supplier quality?
<--- Score

270. Do you allow right of access by your organization, the customer and regulatory authorities to all facilities involved in the order and to all applicable records?
<--- Score

271. What are TQM practices really going on in libyan organizations?
<--- Score

272. Were lessons learned captured and communicated?
<--- Score

273. Are agreed quality levels of deliverables proven?
<--- Score

274. What happens when a new employee joins the organization?
<--- Score

275. How does top management demonstrate leadership and commitment to the QMS?
<--- Score

276. What threat is Supplier Quality Management addressing?
<--- Score

277. Did you have a person in the suppliers facility to observe the suppliers work?
<--- Score

278. If you do not follow, then how to lead?
<--- Score

279. Is the effectiveness of the subcontractors quality assurance system assessed?
<--- Score

280. Is periodic management review addressed and practiced?
<--- Score

281. Is your service Quality vulnerable to supplier cycle-time variations?
<--- Score

Add up total points for this section:
_____ = Total points for this section

Divided by: ______ (number of statements answered) = ______ Average score for this section

Transfer your score to the Supplier Quality Management Index at the beginning of the Self-Assessment.

Supplier Quality Management and Managing Projects, Criteria for Project Managers:

1.0 Initiating Process Group: Supplier Quality Management

1. At which cmmi level are software processes documented, standardized, and integrated into a standard to-be practiced process for your organization?

2. For technology Supplier Quality Management projects only: Are all production support stakeholders (Business unit, technical support, & user) prepared for implementation with appropriate contingency plans?

3. Establishment of pm office?

4. Have you evaluated the teams performance and asked for feedback?

5. Do you know all the stakeholders impacted by the Supplier Quality Management project and what needs are?

6. How well did the chosen processes produce the expected results?

7. How well did you do?

8. At which stage, in a typical Supplier Quality Management project do stake holders have maximum influence?

9. If the risk event occurs, what will you do?

10. What are the short and long term implications?

11. During which stage of Risk planning are risks prioritized based on probability and impact?

12. Who is funding the Supplier Quality Management project?

13. Have the stakeholders identified all individual requirements pertaining to business process?

14. Are you just doing busywork to pass the time?

15. How well did the chosen processes fit the needs of the Supplier Quality Management project?

16. What are the inputs required to produce the deliverables?

17. Where must it be done?

18. Do you know the roles & responsibilities required for this Supplier Quality Management project?

19. Who does what?

20. How can you make your needs known?

1.1 Project Charter: Supplier Quality Management

21. Run it as as a startup?

22. What does it need to do?

23. Why is a Supplier Quality Management project Charter used?

24. What is the justification?

25. Did your Supplier Quality Management project ask for this?

26. What material?

27. Supplier Quality Management project deliverables: what is the Supplier Quality Management project going to produce?

28. Why do you manage integration?

29. Avoid costs, improve service, and/ or comply with a mandate?

30. What barriers do you predict to your success?

31. What is the business need?

32. What is the purpose of the Supplier Quality Management project?

33. What are the known stakeholder requirements?

34. Strategic fit: what is the strategic initiative identifier for this Supplier Quality Management project?

35. What is the most common tool for helping define the detail?

36. Pop quiz – which are the same inputs as in the Supplier Quality Management project charter?

37. What are you striving to accomplish (measurable goal(s))?

38. Who is the sponsor?

39. Supplier Quality Management project objective statement: what must the Supplier Quality Management project do?

40. Are you building in-house ?

1.2 Stakeholder Register: Supplier Quality Management

41. What & Why?

42. Who are the stakeholders?

43. What is the power of the stakeholder?

44. Who wants to talk about Security?

45. Who is managing stakeholder engagement?

46. How should employers make voices heard?

47. How will reports be created?

48. What are the major Supplier Quality Management project milestones requiring communications or providing communications opportunities?

49. What opportunities exist to provide communications?

50. Is your organization ready for change?

51. How much influence do they have on the Supplier Quality Management project?

52. How big is the gap?

1.3 Stakeholder Analysis Matrix: Supplier Quality Management

53. What could your organization improve?

54. Who influences whom?

55. Environmental effects?

56. How can you counter negative efforts?

57. Management cover, succession?

58. Processes, systems, it, communications?

59. Who is most dependent on the resources at stake?

60. Who will promote/support the Supplier Quality Management project, provided that they are involved?

61. Organizational Applicability?

62. Why do you need to manage Supplier Quality Management project Risk?

63. Accreditations, qualifications, certifications?

64. Are there two or three that rise to the top, and a couple that are sliding to the bottom?

65. Technology development and innovation?

66. Beneficiaries; who are the potential beneficiaries?

67. Do the stakeholders goals and expectations support or conflict with the Supplier Quality Management project goals?

68. Inoculations or payment to receive them?

69. What unique or lowest-cost resources does the Supplier Quality Management project have access to?

70. It developments?

71. Is there a reason why you are or are not not using an external rating system?

72. Who is most interested in information about the topic and/or has previously initiated interest?

2.0 Planning Process Group: Supplier Quality Management

73. How does activity resource estimation affect activity duration estimation?

74. Why do it Supplier Quality Management projects fail?

75. Are the necessary foundations in place to ensure the sustainability of the results of the Supplier Quality Management project?

76. What is the difference between the early schedule and late schedule?

77. In which Supplier Quality Management project management process group is the detailed Supplier Quality Management project budget created?

78. What do they need to know about the Supplier Quality Management project?

79. Is the duration of the program sufficient to ensure a cycle that will Supplier Quality Management project the sustainability of the interventions?

80. Is the schedule for the set products being met?

81. To what extent do the intervention objectives and strategies of the Supplier Quality Management project respond to your organizations plans?

82. How can you tell when you are done?

83. Does it make any difference if you are successful?

84. How should needs be met?

85. How will you do it?

86. To what extent is the program helping to influence your organizations policy framework?

87. To what extent are the participating departments coordinating with each other?

88. Why is it important to determine activity sequencing on Supplier Quality Management projects?

89. How well did the chosen processes fit the needs of the Supplier Quality Management project?

90. What is the critical path for this Supplier Quality Management project, and what is the duration of the critical path?

91. What do you need to do?

92. Do the partners have sufficient financial capacity to keep up the benefits produced by the programme?

2.1 Project Management Plan: Supplier Quality Management

93. Does the implementation plan have an appropriate division of responsibilities?

94. What went wrong?

95. What data/reports/tools/etc. do program managers need?

96. What is risk management?

97. What is Supplier Quality Management project scope management?

98. If the Supplier Quality Management project management plan is a comprehensive document that guides you in Supplier Quality Management project execution and control, then what should it NOT contain?

99. Does the selected plan protect privacy?

100. How can you best help your organization to develop consistent practices in Supplier Quality Management project management planning stages?

101. Who is the Supplier Quality Management project Manager?

102. What did not work so well?

103. How well are you able to manage your risk?

104. Is the budget realistic?

105. Are there non-structural buyout or relocation recommendations?

106. Do there need to be organizational changes?

107. Why Change?

108. Where does all this information come from?

109. How do you manage time?

110. What data/reports/tools/etc. do your PMs need?

111. Is the engineering content at a feasibility level-of-detail, and is it sufficiently complete, to provide an adequate basis for the baseline cost estimate?

2.2 Scope Management Plan: Supplier Quality Management

112. Has stakeholder analysis been conducted, assessing influence on the Supplier Quality Management project and authority levels?

113. Materials available for performing the work?

114. Have external dependencies been captured in the schedule?

115. Is your organization structure for both tracking & controlling the budget well defined and assigned to a specific individual?

116. Are software metrics formally captured, analyzed and used as a basis for other Supplier Quality Management project estimates?

117. What are the risks that could significantly affect procuring consultant staff for the Supplier Quality Management project?

118. What is the unique product, service or result?

119. Are there procedures in place to effectively manage interdependencies with other Supplier Quality Management projects, systems, Vendors and your organizations work effort?

120. Does the quality assurance process provide objective verification of adherence to applicable

standards, procedures & requirements?

121. Has a structured approach been used to break work effort into manageable components (WBS)?

122. What are the risks that could significantly affect the schedule of the Supplier Quality Management project?

123. Are issues raised, assessed, actioned, and resolved in a timely and efficient manner?

124. Personnel with expertise?

125. Are funding resource estimates sufficiently detailed and documented for use in planning and tracking the Supplier Quality Management project?

126. When will scope verification be performed?

127. Has a resource management plan been created?

128. Are tasks tracked by hours?

129. Has a provision been made to reassess Supplier Quality Management project risks at various Supplier Quality Management project stages?

130. Staffing Requirements?

131. Has the selected plan been formulated using cost effectiveness and incremental analysis techniques?

2.3 Requirements Management Plan: Supplier Quality Management

132. Do you expect stakeholders to be cooperative?

133. Will you perform a Requirements Risk assessment and develop a plan to deal with risks?

134. What cost metrics will be used?

135. How do you know that you have done this right?

136. Do you understand the role that each stakeholder will play in the requirements process?

137. Is there formal agreement on who has authority to request a change in requirements?

138. Who is responsible for quantifying the Supplier Quality Management project requirements?

139. Do you know which stakeholders will participate in the requirements effort?

140. Did you avoid subjective, flowery or non-specific statements?

141. Will you use tracing to help understand the impact of a change in requirements?

142. Did you provide clear and concise specifications?

143. In case of software development; Should you

have a test for each code module?

144. Did you get proper approvals?

145. Who will perform the analysis?

146. How will requirements be managed?

147. Did you distinguish the scope of work the contractor(s) will be required to do?

148. How will you develop the schedule of requirements activities?

149. Will the Supplier Quality Management project requirements become approved in writing?

150. How often will the reporting occur?

151. What went right?

2.4 Requirements Documentation: Supplier Quality Management

152. Do your constraints stand?

153. What marketing channels do you want to use: e-mail, letter or sms?

154. Can the requirements be checked?

155. What kind of entity is a problem ?

156. What is the risk associated with the technology?

157. If applicable; are there issues linked with the fact that this is an offshore Supplier Quality Management project?

158. How does the proposed Supplier Quality Management project contribute to the overall objectives of your organization?

159. Does your organization restrict technical alternatives?

160. Who provides requirements?

161. Is your business case still valid?

162. Does the system provide the functions which best support the customers needs?

163. Are all functions required by the customer

included?

164. How do you get the user to tell you what they want?

165. How linear / iterative is your Requirements Gathering process (or will it be)?

166. What are current process problems?

167. What variations exist for a process?

168. Has requirements gathering uncovered information that would necessitate changes?

169. How will they be documented / shared?

170. Where do system and software requirements come from, what are sources?

171. Basic work/business process; high-level, what is being touched?

2.5 Requirements Traceability Matrix: Supplier Quality Management

172. What are the chronologies, contingencies, consequences, criteria?

173. Will you use a Requirements Traceability Matrix?

174. Do you have a clear understanding of all subcontracts in place?

175. How will it affect the stakeholders personally in career?

176. Is there a requirements traceability process in place?

177. How do you manage scope?

178. Why do you manage scope?

179. What percentage of Supplier Quality Management projects are producing traceability matrices between requirements and other work products?

180. How small is small enough?

181. Why use a WBS?

182. Describe the process for approving requirements so they can be added to the traceability matrix and Supplier Quality Management project work can be

performed. Will the Supplier Quality Management project requirements become approved in writing?

183. What is the WBS?

2.6 Project Scope Statement: Supplier Quality Management

184. Are there completion/verification criteria defined for each task producing an output?

185. Which risks does the Supplier Quality Management project focus on?

186. Have the reports to be produced, distributed, and filed been defined?

187. Is the plan under configuration management?

188. Is there an information system for the Supplier Quality Management project?

189. Is there a baseline plan against which to measure progress?

190. Were key Supplier Quality Management project stakeholders brought into the Supplier Quality Management project Plan?

191. If there are vendors, have they signed off on the Supplier Quality Management project Plan?

192. Do you anticipate new stakeholders joining the Supplier Quality Management project over time?

193. How often will scope changes be reviewed?

194. Is the Supplier Quality Management project

manager qualified and experienced in Supplier Quality Management project management?

195. Will you need a statement of work?

196. Is there a process (test plans, inspections, reviews) defined for verifying outputs for each task?

197. Are there backup strategies for key members of the Supplier Quality Management project?

198. What are the major deliverables of the Supplier Quality Management project?

199. Elements that deal with providing the detail?

200. What is a process you might recommend to verify the accuracy of the research deliverable?

201. Will statistics related to QA be collected, trends analyzed, and problems raised as issues?

202. Write a brief purpose statement for this Supplier Quality Management project. Include a business justification statement. What is the product of this Supplier Quality Management project?

203. Has a method and process for requirement tracking been developed?

2.7 Assumption and Constraint Log: Supplier Quality Management

204. Do documented requirements exist for all critical components and areas, including technical, business, interfaces, performance, security and conversion requirements?

205. If appropriate, is the deliverable content consistent with current Supplier Quality Management project documents and in compliance with the Document Management Plan?

206. Are there processes defining how software will be developed including development methods, overall timeline for development, software product standards, and traceability?

207. Is there a Steering Committee in place?

208. What worked well?

209. When can log be discarded?

210. Have adequate resources been provided by management to ensure Supplier Quality Management project success?

211. Are you meeting your customers expectations consistently?

212. Are there standards for code development?

213. Are there nonconformance issues?

214. How relevant is this attribute to this Supplier Quality Management project or audit?

215. Are there processes in place to ensure internal consistency between the source code components?

216. Is there adequate stakeholder participation for the vetting of requirements definition, changes and management?

217. Can you perform this task or activity in a more effective manner?

218. Is there documentation of system capability requirements, data requirements, environment requirements, security requirements, and computer and hardware requirements?

219. What does an audit system look like?

220. No superfluous information or marketing narrative?

221. Does the system design reflect the requirements?

222. Has a Supplier Quality Management project Communications Plan been developed?

223. Is the amount of effort justified by the anticipated value of forming a new process?

2.8 Work Breakdown Structure: Supplier Quality Management

224. How far down?

225. When does it have to be done?

226. How much detail?

227. What has to be done?

228. How big is a work-package?

229. What is the probability that the Supplier Quality Management project duration will exceed xx weeks?

230. Can you make it?

231. When do you stop?

232. What is the probability of completing the Supplier Quality Management project in less that xx days?

233. Who has to do it?

234. Why would you develop a Work Breakdown Structure?

235. Where does it take place?

236. Is it a change in scope?

237. Is it still viable?

238. Do you need another level?

239. How will you and your Supplier Quality Management project team define the Supplier Quality Management projects scope and work breakdown structure?

2.9 WBS Dictionary: Supplier Quality Management

240. Does the contractor require sufficient detailed planning of control accounts to constrain the application of budget initially allocated for future effort to current effort?

241. Are retroactive changes to budgets for completed work specifically prohibited in an established procedure, and is this procedure adhered to?

242. Major functional areas of contract effort?

243. Budgeted cost for work performed?

244. All cwbs elements specified for external reporting?

245. Are overhead cost budgets established for each organization which has authority to incur overhead costs?

246. Are overhead cost budgets (or Supplier Quality Management projections) established on a facility-wide basis at least annually for the life of the contract?

247. Where learning is used in developing underlying budgets is there a direct relationship between anticipated learning and time phased budgets?

248. Are management actions taken to reduce

indirect costs when there are significant adverse variances?

249. Is cost and schedule performance measurement done in a consistent, systematic manner?

250. Budgets assigned to major functional organizations?

251. What is the goal?

252. The total budget for the contract (including estimates for authorized and unpriced work)?

253. Are indirect costs accumulated for comparison with the corresponding budgets?

254. Are current work performance indicators and goals relatable to original goals as modified by contractual changes, replanning, and reprogramming actions?

255. Changes in the direct base to which overhead costs are allocated?

256. Where engineering standards or other internal work measurement systems are used, is there a formal relationship between corresponding values and work package budgets?

257. Are all elements of indirect expense identified to overhead cost budgets of Supplier Quality Management projections?

2.10 Schedule Management Plan: Supplier Quality Management

258. What does a valid Schedule look like?

259. Has the ims been resource-loaded and are assigned resources reasonable and available?

260. Are schedule performance measures defined including pre-set triggers for specific actions?

261. Is the schedule feasible and at what cost?

262. Is the ims development and management approach described?

263. Are updated Supplier Quality Management project time & resource estimates reasonable based on the current Supplier Quality Management project stage?

264. Are procurement deliverables arriving on time and to specification?

265. Does the business case include how the Supplier Quality Management project aligns with your organizations strategic goals & objectives?

266. Have Supplier Quality Management project management standards and procedures been identified / established and documented?

267. Why time management?

268. Are the constraints or deadlines associated with the task accurate?

269. Is there an approved case?

270. Supplier Quality Management project definition & scope?

271. Time for overtime?

272. What threats might prevent you from getting there?

273. What weaknesses do you have?

274. Are vendor invoices audited for accuracy before payment?

275. What will be the final cost of the Supplier Quality Management project if status quo is maintained?

2.11 Activity List: Supplier Quality Management

276. In what sequence?

277. Is infrastructure setup part of your Supplier Quality Management project?

278. What are you counting on?

279. How do you determine the late start (LS) for each activity?

280. What did not go as well?

281. Can you determine the activity that must finish, before this activity can start?

282. When will the work be performed?

283. How can the Supplier Quality Management project be displayed graphically to better visualize the activities?

284. Is there anything planned that does not need to be here?

285. Should you include sub-activities?

286. What is the LF and LS for each activity?

287. What is the probability the Supplier Quality Management project can be completed in xx weeks?

288. When do the individual activities need to start and finish?

289. What will be performed?

290. What went well?

291. How difficult will it be to do specific activities on this Supplier Quality Management project?

292. For other activities, how much delay can be tolerated?

293. Are the required resources available or need to be acquired?

2.12 Activity Attributes: Supplier Quality Management

294. Activity: what is In the Bag?

295. What conclusions/generalizations can you draw from this?

296. What is missing?

297. Has management defined a definite timeframe for the turnaround or Supplier Quality Management project window?

298. How difficult will it be to complete specific activities on this Supplier Quality Management project?

299. Resources to accomplish the work?

300. Resource is assigned to?

301. How much activity detail is required?

302. Does your organization of the data change its meaning?

303. Have constraints been applied to the start and finish milestones for the phases?

304. Which method produces the more accurate cost assignment?

305. How difficult will it be to do specific activities on this Supplier Quality Management project?

306. Can more resources be added?

307. Activity: what is Missing?

308. What is the general pattern here?

309. What activity do you think you should spend the most time on?

2.13 Milestone List: Supplier Quality Management

310. When will the Supplier Quality Management project be complete?

311. Effects on core activities, distraction?

312. How late can each activity be finished and started?

313. It is to be a narrative text providing the crucial aspects of your Supplier Quality Management project proposal answering what, who, how, when and where?

314. Vital contracts and partners?

315. Can you derive how soon can the whole Supplier Quality Management project finish?

316. Continuity, supply chain robustness?

317. Sustainable financial backing?

318. Own known vulnerabilities?

319. Legislative effects?

320. Marketing - reach, distribution, awareness?

321. Obstacles faced?

322. What has been done so far?

323. Gaps in capabilities?

324. How will the milestone be verified?

325. How will you get the word out to customers?

326. Milestone pages should display the UserID of the person who added the milestone. Does a report or query exist that provides this audit information?

327. Competitive advantages?

2.14 Network Diagram: Supplier Quality Management

328. What activities must occur simultaneously with this activity?

329. What are the Key Success Factors?

330. Where do you schedule uncertainty time?

331. What are the tools?

332. What activities must follow this activity?

333. What controls the start and finish of a job?

334. Are you on time?

335. Exercise: what is the probability that the Supplier Quality Management project duration will exceed xx weeks?

336. How difficult will it be to do specific activities on this Supplier Quality Management project?

337. Are the required resources available?

338. What to do and When?

339. What job or jobs could run concurrently?

340. Are the gantt chart and/or network diagram updated periodically and used to assess the overall

Supplier Quality Management project timetable?

341. What activity must be completed immediately before this activity can start?

342. What job or jobs precede it?

343. Planning: who, how long, what to do?

344. If x is long, what would be the completion time if you break x into two parallel parts of y weeks and z weeks?

345. Review the logical flow of the network diagram. Take a look at which activities you have first and then sequence the activities. Do they make sense?

346. What are the Major Administrative Issues?

347. Can you calculate the confidence level?

2.15 Activity Resource Requirements: Supplier Quality Management

348. Which logical relationship does the PDM use most often?

349. Do you use tools like decomposition and rolling-wave planning to produce the activity list and other outputs?

350. When does monitoring begin?

351. Anything else?

352. What is the Work Plan Standard?

353. How many signatures do you require on a check and does this match what is in your policy and procedures?

354. Other support in specific areas?

355. What are constraints that you might find during the Human Resource Planning process?

356. Are there unresolved issues that need to be addressed?

357. Why do you do that?

358. How do you handle petty cash?

2.16 Resource Breakdown Structure: Supplier Quality Management

359. Who will be used as a Supplier Quality Management project team member?

360. What defines a successful Supplier Quality Management project?

361. What is the purpose of assigning and documenting responsibility?

362. What are the requirements for resource data?

363. What is your organizations history in doing similar activities?

364. What is the number one predictor of a groups productivity?

365. When do they need the information?

366. Why do you do it?

367. Why is this important?

368. What is each stakeholders desired outcome for the Supplier Quality Management project?

369. Is predictive resource analysis being done?

370. What defines a successful Supplier Quality Management project?

371. Goals for the Supplier Quality Management project. What is each stakeholders desired outcome for the Supplier Quality Management project?

372. The list could probably go on, but, the thing that you would most like to know is, How long & How much?

373. What is the primary purpose of the human resource plan?

2.17 Activity Duration Estimates: Supplier Quality Management

374. Is a contract developed which obligates the seller and the buyer?

375. How much time is required to develop it?

376. Are operational definitions created to identify quality measurement criteria for specific activities?

377. Which is a benefit of an analogous Supplier Quality Management project estimate?

378. When would a milestone chart be used instead of a bar char?

379. How can organizations use a weighted decision matrix to evaluate proposals as part of source selection?

380. Account for the make-or-buy process and how to perform the financial calculations involved in the process. What are the main types of contracts if you do decide to outsource?

381. What are the ways to create and distribute Supplier Quality Management project performance information?

382. Are updates on work results collected and used as inputs to the performance reporting process?

383. Calculate the expected duration for an activity that has a most likely time of 5, a pessimistic time of 13, and a optimiztic time of 3?

384. Consider the changes in the job market for information technology workers. How does the job market and current state of the economy affect human resource management?

385. Which types of reports would help provide summary information to senior management?

386. Does a process exist for approving or rejecting changes?

387. Which is the BEST thing to do to try to complete a Supplier Quality Management project two days earlier?

388. When a risk event occurs, is the risk response evaluated and the appropriate response implemented?

389. Are procedures followed to ensure information is available to stakeholders in a timely manner?

390. Is a provider selected based upon defined evaluation criteria?

391. What distinguishes one organization from another in this area?

392. Explanation notice how many choices are half right?

393. Does a process exist to determine the potential

loss or gain if risk events occur?

2.18 Duration Estimating Worksheet: Supplier Quality Management

394. Does the Supplier Quality Management project provide innovative ways for stakeholders to overcome obstacles or deliver better outcomes?

395. Can the Supplier Quality Management project be constructed as planned?

396. What is your role?

397. Is this operation cost effective?

398. Why estimate time and cost?

399. What utility impacts are there?

400. What info is needed?

401. How should ongoing costs be monitored to try to keep the Supplier Quality Management project within budget?

402. What is next?

403. Will the Supplier Quality Management project collaborate with the local community and leverage resources?

404. What is an Average Supplier Quality Management project?

405. What are the critical bottleneck activities?

406. Define the work as completely as possible. What work will be included in the Supplier Quality Management project?

407. What questions do you have?

408. Science = process: remember the scientific method?

409. When, then?

410. Is the Supplier Quality Management project responsive to community need?

411. What work will be included in the Supplier Quality Management project?

2.19 Project Schedule: Supplier Quality Management

412. How can you shorten the schedule?

413. What is the purpose of a Supplier Quality Management project schedule?

414. What does that mean?

415. Are you working on the right risks?

416. Your Supplier Quality Management project management plan results in a Supplier Quality Management project schedule that is too long. If the Supplier Quality Management project network diagram cannot change and you have extra personnel resources, what is the BEST thing to do?

417. Month Supplier Quality Management project take?

418. Did the Supplier Quality Management project come in under budget?

419. Understand the constraints used in preparing the schedule. Are activities connected because logic dictates the order in which others occur?

420. Does the condition or event threaten the Supplier Quality Management projects objectives in any ways?

421. How do you manage Supplier Quality Management project Risk?

422. Why is software Supplier Quality Management project disaster so common?

423. Is infrastructure setup part of your Supplier Quality Management project?

424. Is Supplier Quality Management project work proceeding in accordance with the original Supplier Quality Management project schedule?

425. Supplier Quality Management project work estimates Who is managing the work estimate quality of work tasks in the Supplier Quality Management project schedule?

426. Is the structure for tracking the Supplier Quality Management project schedule well defined and assigned to a specific individual?

427. Have all Supplier Quality Management project delays been adequately accounted for, communicated to all stakeholders and adjustments made in overall Supplier Quality Management project schedule?

428. Are procedures defined by which the Supplier Quality Management project schedule may be changed?

429. Are key risk mitigation strategies added to the Supplier Quality Management project schedule?

430. Why is this particularly bad?

2.20 Cost Management Plan: Supplier Quality Management

431. How do you manage cost?

432. What is cost and Supplier Quality Management project cost management?

433. Mitigation – based on the action, cost and probability of success, will the mitigation be made?

434. What would you do differently what did not work?

435. Have the reasons why the changes to your organizational systems and capabilities are required?

436. Is there any form of automated support for Issues Management?

437. Timeline and milestones?

438. Is documentation created for communication with the suppliers and Vendors?

439. Cost / benefit analysis?

440. Has the business need been clearly defined?

441. Are cause and effect determined for risks when others occur?

442. Are actuals compared against estimates to

analyze and correct variances?

443. Does a documented Supplier Quality Management project organizational policy & plan (i.e. governance model) exist?

444. Is Supplier Quality Management project work proceeding in accordance with the original Supplier Quality Management project schedule?

445. Cost tracking and performance analysis – How will cost tracking and performance analysis be accomplished?

446. Are all key components of a Quality Assurance Plan present?

447. Is the quality assurance team identified?

448. Are any non-compliance issues that exist due to State practices communicated to your organization?

449. Owner, contractor, and subcontractors?

450. Are vendor contract reports, reviews and visits conducted periodically?

2.21 Activity Cost Estimates: Supplier Quality Management

451. Who determines the quality and expertise of contractors?

452. How do you fund change orders?

453. What defines a successful Supplier Quality Management project?

454. Certification of actual expenditures?

455. Will you need to provide essential services information about activities?

456. Who & what determines the need for contracted services?

457. Does the estimator estimate by task or by person?

458. Where can you get activity reports?

459. Are data needed on characteristics of care?

460. Based on your Supplier Quality Management project communication management plan, what worked well?

461. How do you allocate indirect costs to activities?

462. Performance bond should always provide what

part of the contract value?

463. Can you delete activities or make them inactive?

464. How and when do you enter into Supplier Quality Management project Procurement Management?

465. What cost data should be used to estimate costs during the 2-year follow-up period?

466. Were the tasks or work products prepared by the consultant useful?

467. What were things that you need to improve?

468. What makes a good expected result statement?

469. How many activities should you have?

2.22 Cost Estimating Worksheet: Supplier Quality Management

470. Can a trend be established from historical performance data on the selected measure and are the criteria for using trend analysis or forecasting methods met?

471. What happens to any remaining funds not used?

472. Will the Supplier Quality Management project collaborate with the local community and leverage resources?

473. What costs are to be estimated?

474. Identify the timeframe necessary to monitor progress and collect data to determine how the selected measure has changed?

475. Is the Supplier Quality Management project responsive to community need?

476. How will the results be shared and to whom?

477. What is the purpose of estimating?

478. What can be included?

479. What will others want?

480. Does the Supplier Quality Management project provide innovative ways for stakeholders to overcome

obstacles or deliver better outcomes?

481. Who is best positioned to know and assist in identifying corresponding factors?

482. Value pocket identification & quantification what are value pockets?

483. What is the estimated labor cost today based upon this information?

484. Is it feasible to establish a control group arrangement?

485. Ask: are others positioned to know, are others credible, and will others cooperate?

486. What additional Supplier Quality Management project(s) could be initiated as a result of this Supplier Quality Management project?

2.23 Cost Baseline: Supplier Quality Management

487. Is the requested change request a result of changes in other Supplier Quality Management project(s)?

488. Where do changes come from?

489. What is the most important thing to do next to make your Supplier Quality Management project successful?

490. Has the documentation relating to operation and maintenance of the product(s) or service(s) been delivered to, and accepted by, operations management?

491. What is cost and Supplier Quality Management project cost management?

492. Vac -variance at completion, how much over/ under budget do you expect to be?

493. Has training and knowledge transfer of the operations organization been completed?

494. On time?

495. How long are you willing to wait before you find out were late?

496. Are procedures defined by which the cost

baseline may be changed?

497. Has the Supplier Quality Management project documentation been archived or otherwise disposed as described in the Supplier Quality Management project communication plan?

498. Have the resources used by the Supplier Quality Management project been reassigned to other units or Supplier Quality Management projects?

499. How likely is it to go wrong?

500. Is request in line with priorities?

501. Is there anything you need from upper management in order to be successful?

502. What is your organizations history in doing similar tasks?

503. Has the actual cost of the Supplier Quality Management project (or Supplier Quality Management project phase) been tallied and compared to the approved budget?

504. Definition of done can be traced back to the definitions of what are you providing to the customer in terms of deliverables?

505. Have all approved changes to the schedule baseline been identified and impact on the Supplier Quality Management project documented?

2.24 Quality Management Plan: Supplier Quality Management

506. Is it necessary?

507. How do you decide what information to record?

508. Have Supplier Quality Management project management standards and procedures been established and documented?

509. Were there any deficiencies / issues identified in the prior years self-assessment?

510. How many Supplier Quality Management project staff does this specific process affect?

511. How does training support what is important to your organization and the individual?

512. Does the plan conform to standards?

513. What has the QM Collaboration done?

514. How are changes recorded?

515. How does your organization recruit, hire, and retain new employees?

516. Who is responsible?

517. Sampling part of task?

518. List your organizations customer contact standards that employees are expected to maintain. How are corresponding standards measured?

519. How is staff trained on the recording of field notes?

520. How do you decide what information needs to be recorded?

521. Why quality management?

522. Do you periodically review your data quality system to see that it is up to date and appropriate?

523. How are your organizations compensation and recognition approaches and the performance management system used to reinforce high performance?

524. How do you document and correct nonconformances?

525. If it is out of compliance, should the process be amended or should the Plan be amended?

2.25 Quality Metrics: Supplier Quality Management

526. Is the reporting frequency appropriate?

527. Did evaluation start on time?

528. What metrics do you measure?

529. What documentation is required?

530. Have alternatives been defined in the event that failure occurs?

531. Where is quality now?

532. When will the Final Guidance will be issued?

533. Who is willing to lead?

534. What if the biggest risk to your business were the already stated people who do not complain?

535. Is quality culture a competitive advantage?

536. Are applicable standards referenced and available?

537. What are you trying to accomplish?

538. How can the effectiveness of each of the activities be measured?

539. Are there already quality metrics available that detect nonlinear embeddings and trends similar to the users perception?

540. Do you know how much profit a 10% decrease in waste would generate?

541. There are many reasons to shore up quality-related metrics, and what metrics are important?

542. Have risk areas been identified?

543. What method of measurement do you use?

544. Was the overall quality better or worse than previous products?

545. How do you calculate corresponding metrics?

2.26 Process Improvement Plan: Supplier Quality Management

546. The motive is determined by asking, Why do you want to achieve this goal?

547. Management commitment at all levels?

548. What is the test-cycle concept?

549. Are there forms and procedures to collect and record the data?

550. Are you following the quality standards?

551. Are you making progress on your improvement plan?

552. What makes people good SPI coaches?

553. Where do you want to be?

554. Have the frequency of collection and the points in the process where measurements will be made been determined?

555. Are you making progress on the goals?

556. Are you making progress on the improvement framework?

557. Everyone agrees on what process improvement is, right?

558. What lessons have you learned so far?

559. Does explicit definition of the measures exist?

560. How do you manage quality?

561. Does your process ensure quality?

562. To elicit goal statements, do you ask a question such as, What do you want to achieve?

2.27 Responsibility Assignment Matrix: Supplier Quality Management

563. How many hours by each staff member/rate?

564. Identify and isolate causes of favorable and unfavorable cost and schedule variances?

565. The already stated responsible for overhead performance control of related costs?

566. Are overhead costs budgets established on a basis consistent with anticipated direct business base?

567. Are all authorized tasks assigned to identified organizational elements?

568. Is it safe to say you can handle more work or that some tasks you are supposed to do arent worth doing?

569. Does the contractor use objective results, design reviews, and tests to trace schedule?

570. What tool can show you individual and group allocations?

571. Who is going to do that work?

572. The staff characteristics – is the group or the person capable to work together as a team?

573. If a role has only Signing-off, or only Communicating responsibility and has no Performing, Accountable, or Monitoring responsibility, is it necessary?

574. Does the Supplier Quality Management project need to be analyzed further to uncover additional responsibilities?

575. What expertise is available in your department?

576. Are the overhead pools formally and adequately identified?

577. What does wbs accomplish?

2.28 Roles and Responsibilities: Supplier Quality Management

578. Who is responsible for implementation activities and where will the functions, roles and responsibilities be defined?

579. What should you do now to ensure that you are exceeding expectations and excelling in your current position?

580. Does the team have access to and ability to use data analysis tools?

581. How well did the Supplier Quality Management project Team understand the expectations of specific roles and responsibilities?

582. Are governance roles and responsibilities documented?

583. Do you take the time to clearly define roles and responsibilities on Supplier Quality Management project tasks?

584. Required skills, knowledge, experience?

585. Where are you most strong as a supervisor?

586. Once the responsibilities are defined for the Supplier Quality Management project, have the deliverables, roles and responsibilities been clearly communicated to every participant?

587. What specific behaviors did you observe?

588. What should you do now to prepare yourself for a promotion, increased responsibilities or a different job?

589. Who is responsible for each task?

590. What is working well?

591. What expectations were NOT met?

592. Was the expectation clearly communicated?

593. Is there a training program in place for stakeholders covering expectations, roles and responsibilities and any addition knowledge others need to be good stakeholders?

594. What expectations were met?

595. Are your policies supportive of a culture of quality data?

2.29 Human Resource Management Plan: Supplier Quality Management

596. Has a provision been made to reassess Supplier Quality Management project risks at various Supplier Quality Management project stages?

597. Was the Supplier Quality Management project schedule reviewed by all stakeholders and formally accepted?

598. How to convince to employees that it is a necessary process?

599. Are the Supplier Quality Management project plans updated on a frequent basis?

600. Are people being developed to meet the challenges of the future?

601. What are the Staffing Requirements?

602. Is quality monitored from the perspective of the customers needs and expectations?

603. Is an industry recognized support tool(s) being used for Supplier Quality Management project scheduling & tracking?

604. Has a quality assurance plan been developed for the Supplier Quality Management project?

605. Is the communication plan being followed?

606. Are the schedule estimates reasonable given the Supplier Quality Management project?

607. Have all documents been archived in a Supplier Quality Management project repository for each release?

608. What were things that you did well, and could improve, and how?

609. Is there a Quality Management Plan?

610. Measurable - are the targets measurable?

611. Are meeting objectives identified for each meeting?

612. How are you going to ensure that you have a well motivated workforce?

613. Are software metrics formally captured, analyzed and used as a basis for other Supplier Quality Management project estimates?

2.30 Communications Management Plan: Supplier Quality Management

614. Conflict resolution -which method when?

615. What approaches to you feel are the best ones to use?

616. Timing: when do the effects of the communication take place?

617. What communications method?

618. What to know?

619. Which team member will work with each stakeholder?

620. Are you constantly rushing from meeting to meeting?

621. Will messages be directly related to the release strategy or phases of the Supplier Quality Management project?

622. How were corresponding initiatives successful?

623. Who are the members of the governing body?

624. What approaches do you use?

625. Are there potential barriers between the team and the stakeholder?

626. How much time does it take to do it?

627. Do you ask; can you recommend others for you to talk with about this initiative?

628. Who needs to know and how much?

629. Why do you manage communications?

630. How will the person responsible for executing the communication item be notified?

631. What to learn?

2.31 Risk Management Plan: Supplier Quality Management

632. Do you manage the process through use of metrics?

633. Can you stabilize dynamic risk factors?

634. What are the chances the event will occur?

635. What will the damage be?

636. Is the customer willing to commit significant time to the requirements gathering process?

637. Are certain activities taking a long time to complete?

638. Financial risk: can your organization afford to undertake the Supplier Quality Management project?

639. Was an original risk assessment/risk management plan completed?

640. Are the reports useful and easy to read?

641. Why is product liability a serious issue?

642. Prioritized components/features?

643. How can the process be made more effective or less cumbersome (process improvements)?

644. Methodology: how will risk management be performed on this Supplier Quality Management project?

645. Number of users of the product?

646. What risks are tracked?

647. Financial risk -can your organization afford to undertake the Supplier Quality Management project?

648. What are the cost, schedule and resource impacts if the risk does occur?

649. Are there new risks that mitigation strategies might introduce?

650. What can go wrong?

651. What can you do to minimize the impact if it does?

2.32 Risk Register: Supplier Quality Management

652. What is your current and future risk profile?

653. What evidence do you have to justify the likelihood score of the risk (audit, incident report, claim, complaints, inspection, internal review)?

654. Have other controls and solutions been implemented in other services which could be applied as an alternative to additional funding?

655. Is further information required before making a decision?

656. Which key risks have ineffective responses or outstanding improvement actions?

657. What is a Community Risk Register?

658. What could prevent you delivering on the strategic program objectives and what is being done to mitigate corresponding issues?

659. What are the main aims, objectives of the policy, strategy, or service and the intended outcomes?

660. Preventative actions - planned actions to reduce the likelihood a risk will occur and/or reduce the seriousness should it occur. What should you do now?

661. Risk documentation: what reporting formats and

processes will be used for risk management activities?

662. How well are risks controlled?

663. Are there any knock-on effects/impact on any of the other areas?

664. What action, if any, has been taken to respond to the risk?

665. Who is accountable?

666. What are your key risks/show istoppers and what is being done to manage them?

667. Are corrective measures implemented as planned?

668. What may happen or not go according to plan?

669. Amongst the action plans and recommendations that you have to introduce are there some that could stop or delay the overall program?

670. Schedule impact/severity estimated range (workdays) assume the event happens, what is the potential impact?

2.33 Probability and Impact Assessment: Supplier Quality Management

671. When and how will the recent breakthroughs in basic research lead to commercial products?

672. What things might go wrong?

673. Has something like this been done before?

674. What should be the requirement of organizational restructuring as each subSupplier Quality Management project goes through a different lifecycle phase?

675. How will economic events and trends likely affect the Supplier Quality Management project?

676. Management -what contingency plans do you have if the risk becomes a reality?

677. Have decisions that should be left open because of inadequate information on technology been identified and responsibility assigned for reducing the uncertainty?

678. What is the experience (performance, attitude, business ethics, etc.) in the past with contractors?

679. Risk may be made during which step of risk management?

680. What is the risk appetite?

681. How is the risk management process used in practice?

682. Are end-users enthusiastically committed to the Supplier Quality Management project and the system/product to be built?

683. Monitoring of the overall Supplier Quality Management project status – are there any changes in the Supplier Quality Management project that can effect and cause new possible risks?

684. Should the risk be taken at all?

685. What risks does the employee encounter?

686. Is the number of people on the Supplier Quality Management project team adequate to do the job?

687. Are enough people available?

688. Do end-users have realistic expectations?

689. Are requirements fully understood by the software engineering team and customers?

690. Can it be enlarged by drawing people from other areas of your organization?

2.34 Probability and Impact Matrix: Supplier Quality Management

691. Which risks need to move on to Perform Quantitative Risk Analysis?

692. Are tool mentors available?

693. What is the industrial relations prevailing in this organization?

694. How do you analyze the risks in the different types of Supplier Quality Management projects?

695. Which is the BEST thing to do?

696. Economic to take on the Supplier Quality Management project?

697. What needs to be DONE?

698. Lay ground work for future returns?

699. Were there any Supplier Quality Management projects similar to this one in existence?

700. While preparing your risk responses, you identify additional risks. What should you do?

701. Is the technology to be built new to your organization?

702. What will be the impact or consequence if the

risk occurs?

703. Who has experience with this?

704. How carefully have the potential competitors been identified?

705. What should be done with risks on the watch list?

706. What should be the gestation period for the Supplier Quality Management project with this technology?

707. Which role do you have in the Supplier Quality Management project?

708. What are the levels of understanding of the future users of this technology?

2.35 Risk Data Sheet: Supplier Quality Management

709. What is the likelihood of it happening?

710. Has a sensitivity analysis been carried out?

711. What do people affected think about the need for, and practicality of preventive measures?

712. What are the main opportunities available to you that you should grab while you can?

713. Will revised controls lead to tolerable risk levels?

714. What will be the consequences if it happens?

715. How can it happen?

716. How can hazards be reduced?

717. What is the environment within which you operate (social trends, economic, community values, broad based participation, national directions etc.)?

718. Has the most cost-effective solution been chosen?

719. What are your core values?

720. Type of risk identified?

721. Do effective diagnostic tests exist?

722. If it happens, what are the consequences?

723. Potential for recurrence?

724. What if client refuses?

725. What were the Causes that contributed?

726. How reliable is the data source?

727. Who has a vested interest in how you perform as your organization (our stakeholders)?

2.36 Procurement Management Plan: Supplier Quality Management

728. Pareto diagrams, statistical sampling, flow charting or trend analysis used quality monitoring?

729. Is there a procurement management plan in place?

730. Do all stakeholders know how to access the PM repository and where to find the Supplier Quality Management project documentation?

731. Are the budget estimates reasonable?

732. Is it standard practice to formally commit stakeholders to the Supplier Quality Management project via agreements?

733. Have all involved Supplier Quality Management project stakeholders and work groups committed to the Supplier Quality Management project?

734. Have the procedures for identifying budget variances been followed?

735. Have the key elements of a coherent Supplier Quality Management project management strategy been established?

736. Are written status reports provided on a designated frequent basis?

737. If standardized procurement documents are needed, where can others be found?

738. Are milestone deliverables effectively tracked and compared to Supplier Quality Management project plan?

739. Is the structure for tracking the Supplier Quality Management project schedule well defined and assigned to a specific individual?

740. Are mitigation strategies identified?

741. Does the Supplier Quality Management project have a formal Supplier Quality Management project Charter?

742. Are meeting minutes captured and sent out after meetings?

743. Has a capability assessment been conducted?

744. What communication items need improvement?

745. Has a provision been made to reassess Supplier Quality Management project risks at various Supplier Quality Management project stages?

746. Are quality metrics defined?

2.37 Source Selection Criteria: Supplier Quality Management

747. Can you prevent comparison of proposals?

748. How much weight should be placed on past performance information?

749. If the costs are normalized, please account for how the normalization is conducted. Is a cost realism analysis used?

750. How should the preproposal conference be conducted?

751. When is it appropriate to issue a DRFP?

752. What does a sample rating scale look like?

753. Have team members been adequately trained?

754. What are open book debriefings?

755. What should clarifications include?

756. Can you reasonably estimate total organization requirements for the coming year?

757. What is the role of counsel in the procurement process?

758. What are the limitations on pre-competitive range communications?

759. What can not be disclosed?

760. Will the technical evaluation factor unnecessarily force the acquisition into a higher-priced market segment?

761. Are types/quantities of material, facilities appropriate?

762. Are evaluators ready to begin this task?

763. How are oral presentations documented?

764. Comparison of each offers prices to the estimated prices -are there significant differences?

765. Can you identify proposed teaming partners and/or subcontractors and consider the nature and extent of proposed involvement in satisfying the Supplier Quality Management project requirements?

766. How do you consolidate reviews and analysis of evaluators?

2.38 Stakeholder Management Plan: Supplier Quality Management

767. Do any protocols apply for records management?

768. Is there a formal set of procedures supporting Stakeholder Management?

769. How much information should be collected?

770. Are the schedule estimates reasonable given the Supplier Quality Management project?

771. Are non-critical path items updated and agreed upon with the teams?

772. What is the drawback in using qualitative Supplier Quality Management project selection techniques?

773. Are risk oriented checklists used during risk identification?

774. Are multiple estimation methods being employed?

775. Has a provision been made to reassess Supplier Quality Management project risks at various Supplier Quality Management project stages?

776. Which impacts could serve as impediments?

777. Are the key elements of a Supplier Quality

Management project Charter present?

778. Is there a formal set of procedures supporting Issues Management?

779. What is the general purpose in defining responsibilities of the already stated affiliated with the Supplier Quality Management project?

780. Are best practices and metrics employed to identify issues, progress, performance, etc.?

781. What is positive about the current process?

782. Are schedule deliverables actually delivered?

783. What methods are to be used for managing and monitoring subcontractors (eg agreements, contracts etc)?

2.39 Change Management Plan: Supplier Quality Management

784. Who will be the change levers?

785. Readiness -what is a successful end state?

786. When does it make sense to customize?

787. What work practices will be affected?

788. What are the dependencies?

789. Have the approved procedures and policies been published?

790. What is the negative impact of communicating too soon or too late?

791. Would you need to tailor a special message for each segment of the audience?

792. Does this change represent a completely new process for your organization, or a different application of an existing process?

793. What risks may occur upfront?

794. Who might be able to help you the most?

795. What new behaviours are required?

796. Do there need to be new channels developed?

797. Do you need a new organization structure?

798. Has an information & communications plan been developed?

799. Identify the current level of skills and knowledge and behaviours of the group that will be impacted on. What prerequisite knowledge do corresponding groups need?

800. What are the specific target groups/audiences that will be impacted by this change?

801. Do you need new systems?

3.0 Executing Process Group: Supplier Quality Management

802. Will additional funds be needed for hardware or software?

803. What areas were overlooked on this Supplier Quality Management project?

804. Why is it important to determine activity sequencing on Supplier Quality Management projects?

805. What does it mean to take a systems view of a Supplier Quality Management project?

806. Are decisions made in a timely manner?

807. What are the critical steps involved in selecting measures and initiatives?

808. What factors are contributing to progress or delay in the achievement of products and results?

809. Do the products created live up to the necessary quality?

810. How can you use Microsoft Supplier Quality Management project and Excel to assist in Supplier Quality Management project risk management?

811. What are the main types of contracts if you do decide to outsource?

812. How will you avoid scope creep?

813. Have operating capacities been created and/or reinforced in partners?

814. Who will provide training?

815. Is the program supported by national and/or local organizations?

816. How do you measure difficulty?

817. Who are the Supplier Quality Management project stakeholders?

818. When do you share the scorecard with managers?

3.1 Team Member Status Report: Supplier Quality Management

819. How does this product, good, or service meet the needs of the Supplier Quality Management project and your organization as a whole?

820. Will the staff do training or is that done by a third party?

821. Are the attitudes of staff regarding Supplier Quality Management project work improving?

822. What specific interest groups do you have in place?

823. Is there evidence that staff is taking a more professional approach toward management of your organizations Supplier Quality Management projects?

824. Are your organizations Supplier Quality Management projects more successful over time?

825. How can you make it practical?

826. Does every department have to have a Supplier Quality Management project Manager on staff?

827. Why is it to be done?

828. Does your organization have the means (staff, money, contract, etc.) to produce or to acquire the product, good, or service?

829. How will resource planning be done?

830. How much risk is involved?

831. Does the product, good, or service already exist within your organization?

832. When a teams productivity and success depend on collaboration and the efficient flow of information, what generally fails them?

833. Do you have an Enterprise Supplier Quality Management project Management Office (EPMO)?

834. How it is to be done?

835. What is to be done?

836. The problem with Reward & Recognition Programs is that the truly deserving people all too often get left out. How can you make it practical?

837. Are the products of your organizations Supplier Quality Management projects meeting customers objectives?

3.2 Change Request: Supplier Quality Management

838. Who needs to approve change requests?

839. Who will perform the change?

840. Why do you want to have a change control system?

841. What are the requirements for urgent changes?

842. How do you get changes (code) out in a timely manner?

843. How fast will change requests be approved?

844. How are the measures for carrying out the change established?

845. For which areas does this operating procedure apply?

846. How many lines of code must be changed to implement the change?

847. Will the change use memory to the extent that other functions will be not have sufficient memory to operate effectively?

848. Change request coordination ?

849. How well do experienced software developers

predict software change?

850. Who is responsible to authorize changes?

851. What needs to be communicated?

852. Will new change requests be acknowledged in a timely manner?

853. What must be taken into consideration when introducing change control programs?

854. Has a formal technical review been conducted to assess technical correctness?

855. Why control change across the life cycle?

856. Are change requests logged and managed?

3.3 Change Log: Supplier Quality Management

857. Is the requested change request a result of changes in other Supplier Quality Management project(s)?

858. How does this relate to the standards developed for specific business processes?

859. Is the submitted change a new change or a modification of a previously approved change?

860. Do the described changes impact on the integrity or security of the system?

861. Does the suggested change request seem to represent a necessary enhancement to the product?

862. Will the Supplier Quality Management project fail if the change request is not executed?

863. When was the request approved?

864. Does the suggested change request represent a desired enhancement to the products functionality?

865. Who initiated the change request?

866. When was the request submitted?

867. How does this change affect scope?

868. Is the change request within Supplier Quality Management project scope?

869. Is this a mandatory replacement?

870. Should a more thorough impact analysis be conducted?

871. How does this change affect the timeline of the schedule?

872. Is the change backward compatible without limitations?

873. Is the change request open, closed or pending?

3.4 Decision Log: Supplier Quality Management

874. What alternatives/risks were considered?

875. What are the cost implications?

876. Is your opponent open to a non-traditional workflow, or will it likely challenge anything you do?

877. Behaviors; what are guidelines that the team has identified that will assist them with getting the most out of team meetings?

878. How do you know when you are achieving it?

879. Decision-making process; how will the team make decisions?

880. How do you define success?

881. It becomes critical to track and periodically revisit both operational effectiveness; Are you noticing all that you need to, and are you interpreting what you see effectively?

882. What is your overall strategy for quality control / quality assurance procedures?

883. How does provision of information, both in terms of content and presentation, influence acceptance of alternative strategies?

884. How does an increasing emphasis on cost containment influence the strategies and tactics used?

885. Who will be given a copy of this document and where will it be kept?

886. How effective is maintaining the log at facilitating organizational learning?

887. Adversarial environment. is your opponent open to a non-traditional workflow, or will it likely challenge anything you do?

888. How consolidated and comprehensive a story can you tell by capturing currently available incident data in a central location and through a log of key decisions during an incident?

889. Who is the decisionmaker?

890. How does the use a Decision Support System influence the strategies/tactics or costs?

891. What eDiscovery problem or issue did your organization set out to fix or make better?

892. Linked to original objective?

893. Does anything need to be adjusted?

3.5 Quality Audit: Supplier Quality Management

894. What happens if your organization fails its Quality Audit?

895. How does your organization know that its system for recruiting the best staff possible are appropriately effective and constructive?

896. How does the organization know that its industry and community engagement planning and management systems are appropriately effective and constructive in enabling relationships with key stakeholder groups?

897. Are there appropriate means for intervening if necessary?

898. What review processes are in place for your organizations major activities?

899. How does your organization know that its system for commercializing research outputs is appropriately effective and constructive?

900. How is the Strategic Plan (and other plans) reviewed and revised?

901. What data about organizational performance is routinely collected and reported?

902. Are people allowed to contribute ideas?

903. Does the report read coherently?

904. If your organization thinks it is doing something well, can it prove this?

905. Are measuring and test equipment that have been placed out of service suitably identified and excluded from use in any device reconditioning operation?

906. Are all staff empowered and encouraged to contribute to ongoing improvement efforts?

907. How does your organization know that its system for attending to the particular needs of its international staff is appropriately effective and constructive?

908. How does your organization know that its staffing profile is optimally aligned with the capability requirements implicit (or explicit) in its Strategic Plan?

909. How does your organization know that its system for ensuring a positive organizational climate is appropriately effective and constructive?

910. Will the evidence likely be sufficient and appropriate?

911. Is your organizational structure established and each positions responsibility defined?

912. How does your organization know that the quality of its supervisors is appropriately effective and constructive?

913. How does your organization know that it is effectively and constructively guiding staff through to timely completion of tasks?

3.6 Team Directory: Supplier Quality Management

914. Where should the information be distributed?

915. When will you produce deliverables?

916. How do unidentified risks impact the outcome of the Supplier Quality Management project?

917. Do purchase specifications and configurations match requirements?

918. How does the team resolve conflicts and ensure tasks are completed?

919. Process decisions: which organizational elements and which individuals will be assigned management functions?

920. Decisions: is the most suitable form of contract being used?

921. Where will the product be used and/or delivered or built when appropriate?

922. Days from the time the issue is identified?

923. Who should receive information (all stakeholders)?

924. Who are the Team Members?

925. Process decisions: are all start-up, turn over and close out requirements of the contract satisfied?

926. How and in what format should information be presented?

927. Who will report Supplier Quality Management project status to all stakeholders?

928. Timing: when do the effects of communication take place?

929. Decisions: what could be done better to improve the quality of the constructed product?

930. Who will write the meeting minutes and distribute?

931. How will you accomplish and manage the objectives?

3.7 Team Operating Agreement: Supplier Quality Management

932. Has the appropriate access to relevant data and analysis capability been granted?

933. Did you determine the technology methods that best match the messages to be communicated?

934. How does teaming fit in with overall organizational goals and meet organizational needs?

935. How will you resolve conflict efficiently and respectfully?

936. Conflict resolution: how will disputes and other conflicts be mediated or resolved?

937. What administrative supports will be put in place to support the team and the teams supervisor?

938. Do you brief absent members after they view meeting notes or listen to a recording?

939. To whom do you deliver your services?

940. Confidentiality: how will confidential information be handled?

941. Are there differences in access to communication and collaboration technology based on team member location?

942. Do you vary your voice pace, tone and pitch to engage participants and gain involvement?

943. What are some potential sources of conflict among team members?

944. What individual strengths does each team member bring to the group?

945. How will you divide work equitably?

946. Does your team need access to all documents and information at all times?

947. Do you use a parking lot for any items that are important and outside of the agenda?

948. What is your unique contribution to your organization?

949. The method to be used in the decision making process; Will it be consensus, majority rule, or the supervisor having the final say?

950. What is a Virtual Team?

3.8 Team Performance Assessment: Supplier Quality Management

951. What do you think is the most constructive thing that could be done now to resolve considerations and disputes about method variance?

952. To what degree will the team ensure that all members equitably share the work essential to the success of the team?

953. To what degree is there a sense that only the team can succeed?

954. To what degree are fresh input and perspectives systematically caught and added (for example, through information and analysis, new members, and senior sponsors)?

955. To what degree can all members engage in open and interactive considerations?

956. Delaying market entry: how long is too long?

957. How do you recognize and praise members for contributions?

958. To what degree are the goals realistic?

959. How hard did you try to make a good selection?

960. To what degree does the teams work approach provide opportunity for members to engage in fact-

based problem solving?

961. Is there a particular method of data analysis that you would recommend as a means of demonstrating that method variance is not of great concern for a given dataset?

962. What are you doing specifically to develop the leaders around you?

963. To what degree will team members, individually and collectively, commit time to help themselves and others learn and develop skills?

964. Individual task proficiency and team process behavior: what is important for team functioning?

965. Lack of method variance in self-reported affect and perceptions at work: Reality or artifact?

966. To what degree are the relative importance and priority of the goals clear to all team members?

967. To what degree does the teams purpose constitute a broader, deeper aspiration than just accomplishing short-term goals?

968. To what degree will the team adopt a concrete, clearly understood, and agreed-upon approach that will result in achievement of the teams goals?

969. How do you manage human resources?

970. To what degree do team members understand one anothers roles and skills?

3.9 Team Member Performance Assessment: Supplier Quality Management

971. Are any governance changes sufficient to impact achievement?

972. What future plans (e.g., modifications) do you have for your program?

973. Goals met?

974. To what degree are the goals ambitious?

975. How do you create a self-sustaining capacity for a collaborative culture?

976. Does the rater (supervisor) have the authority or responsibility to tell an employee that the employees performance is unsatisfactory?

977. To what degree are sub-teams possible or necessary?

978. Does adaptive training work?

979. What innovations (if any) are developed to realize goals?

980. What happens if a team member disagrees with the Job Expectations?

981. How often should assessments be conducted?

982. What evidence supports your decision-making?

983. How do you currently account for your results in the teams achievement?

984. How is assessment information achieved, stored?

985. What resources do you need?

986. What is the Business Management Oversight Process?

987. What steps have you taken to improve performance?

988. To what degree is the team cognizant of small wins to be celebrated along the way?

989. What is a general description of the processes under performance measurement and assessment?

990. What happens if a team member receives a Rating of Unsatisfactory?

3.10 Issue Log: Supplier Quality Management

991. How often do you engage with stakeholders?

992. What help do you and your team need from the stakeholders?

993. What does the stakeholder need from the team?

994. In your work, how much time is spent on stakeholder identification?

995. Are stakeholder roles recognized by your organization?

996. Are they needed?

997. What would have to change?

998. Do you have members of your team responsible for certain stakeholders?

999. What is the status of the issue?

1000. What is the impact on the risks?

1001. What are the stakeholders interrelationships?

1002. What steps can you take for positive relationships?

1003. Why do you manage human resources?

1004. What is the stakeholders level of authority?

1005. Persistence; will users learn a work around or will they be bothered every time?

4.0 Monitoring and Controlling Process Group: Supplier Quality Management

1006. If a risk event occurs, what will you do?

1007. What input will you be required to provide the Supplier Quality Management project team?

1008. How well defined and documented were the Supplier Quality Management project management processes you chose to use?

1009. Did the Supplier Quality Management project team have enough people to execute the Supplier Quality Management project plan?

1010. Are the necessary foundations in place to ensure the sustainability of the results of the programme?

1011. How is agile program management done?

1012. How well did the team follow the chosen processes?

1013. How will staff learn how to use the deliverables?

1014. Mitigate. what will you do to minimize the impact should a risk event occur?

1015. Use: how will they use the information?

1016. How is Agile Supplier Quality Management project Management done?

1017. Are there areas that need improvement?

1018. Propriety: who needs to be involved in the evaluation to be ethical?

1019. Is the program in place as intended?

4.1 Project Performance Report: Supplier Quality Management

1020. To what degree does the task meet individual needs?

1021. To what degree are the skill areas critical to team performance present?

1022. To what degree can team members vigorously define the teams purpose in considerations with others who are not part of the functioning team?

1023. To what degree does the teams work approach provide opportunity for members to engage in open interaction?

1024. What is the degree to which rules govern information exchange between individuals within your organization?

1025. To what degree are the demands of the task compatible with and converge with the mission and functions of the formal organization?

1026. To what degree is the information network consistent with the structure of the formal organization?

1027. To what degree will the approach capitalize on and enhance the skills of all team members in a manner that takes into consideration other demands on members of the team?

1028. To what degree do the goals specify concrete team work products?

1029. To what degree do team members articulate the teams work approach?

1030. To what degree can team members meet frequently enough to accomplish the teams ends?

1031. To what degree does the teams purpose contain themes that are particularly meaningful and memorable?

1032. To what degree do team members feel that the purpose of the team is important, if not exciting?

4.2 Variance Analysis: Supplier Quality Management

1033. Are meaningful indicators identified for use in measuring the status of cost and schedule performance?

1034. How does the use of a single conversion element (rather than the traditional labor and overhead elements) affect standard costing?

1035. How does the monthly budget compare to the actual experience?

1036. What are the actual costs to date?

1037. There are detailed schedules which support control account and work package start and completion dates/events?

1038. Are there knowledgeable Supplier Quality Management projections of future performance?

1039. Did an existing competitor change strategy?

1040. Does the contractors system include procedures for measuring the performance of critical subcontractors?

1041. Historical experience?

1042. Does the contractor use objective results, design reviews and tests to trace schedule performance?

1043. Can process improvements lead to unfavorable variances?

1044. Is work progressively subdivided into detailed work packages as requirements are defined?

1045. Is the anticipated (firm and potential) business base Supplier Quality Management projected in a rational, consistent manner?

1046. Why do variances exist?

1047. How do you evaluate the impact of schedule changes, work around, et?

1048. Are there quarterly budgets with quarterly performance comparisons?

1049. Contract line items and end items?

1050. What is the actual cost of work performed?

4.3 Earned Value Status: Supplier Quality Management

1051. Earned value can be used in almost any Supplier Quality Management project situation and in almost any Supplier Quality Management project environment. it may be used on large Supplier Quality Management projects, medium sized Supplier Quality Management projects, tiny Supplier Quality Management projects (in cut-down form), complex and simple Supplier Quality Management projects and in any market sector. some people, of course, know all about earned value, they have used it for years - but perhaps not as effectively as they could have?

1052. Verification is a process of ensuring that the developed system satisfies the stakeholders agreements and specifications; Are you building the product right? What do you verify?

1053. Where are your problem areas?

1054. What is the unit of forecast value?

1055. How does this compare with other Supplier Quality Management projects?

1056. Where is evidence-based earned value in your organization reported?

1057. Validation is a process of ensuring that the developed system will actually achieve the stakeholders desired outcomes; Are you building the right product? What do you validate?

1058. Are you hitting your Supplier Quality Management projects targets?

1059. How much is it going to cost by the finish?

1060. When is it going to finish?

1061. If earned value management (EVM) is so good in determining the true status of a Supplier Quality Management project and Supplier Quality Management project its completion, why is it that hardly any one uses it in information systems related Supplier Quality Management projects?

4.4 Risk Audit: Supplier Quality Management

1062. What expertise do auditors need to generate effective business-level risk assessments, and to what extent do auditors currently possess the already stated attributes?

1063. For paid staff, does your organization comply with the minimum conditions for employment and/or the applicable modern award?

1064. Has everyone (staff, volunteers and participants) agreed to a code of behaviour or conduct?

1065. How do you govern assets?

1066. Are requirements fully understood by the team and customers?

1067. Do you have an understanding of insurance claims processes?

1068. What risk does not having unique identification present?

1069. Are the software tools integrated with each other?

1070. Do you have a realistic budget and do you present regular financial reports that identify how you are going against that budget?

1071. Does the customer have a solid idea of what is required?

1072. Do requirements demand the use of new analysis, design, or testing methods?

1073. Will safety checks of personal equipment supplied by competitors be conducted?

1074. To what extent are auditors influenced by the business risk assessment in the audit process, and how can auditors create more effective mental models to more fully examine contradictory evidence?

1075. When your organization is entering into a major contract, does it seek legal advice?

1076. Do you have proper induction processes for all new paid staff and volunteers who have a specific role and responsibility?

1077. Are you aware of the industry standards that apply to your operations?

1078. Are contracts reviewed before renewal?

1079. Do you have a procedure for dealing with complaints?

1080. Are Supplier Quality Management project requirements stable?

4.5 Contractor Status Report: Supplier Quality Management

1081. What was the budget or estimated cost for your organizations services?

1082. What process manages the contracts?

1083. What was the actual budget or estimated cost for your organizations services?

1084. How long have you been using the services?

1085. Are there contractual transfer concerns?

1086. How does the proposed individual meet each requirement?

1087. What was the final actual cost?

1088. Describe how often regular updates are made to the proposed solution. Are corresponding regular updates included in the standard maintenance plan?

1089. What are the minimum and optimal bandwidth requirements for the proposed solution?

1090. What was the overall budget or estimated cost?

1091. Who can list a Supplier Quality Management project as organization experience, your organization or a previous employee of your organization?

1092. If applicable; describe your standard schedule for new software version releases. Are new software version releases included in the standard maintenance plan?

1093. What is the average response time for answering a support call?

1094. How is risk transferred?

4.6 Formal Acceptance: Supplier Quality Management

1095. How well did the team follow the methodology?

1096. What can you do better next time?

1097. Do you perform formal acceptance or burn-in tests?

1098. What was done right?

1099. Does it do what Supplier Quality Management project team said it would?

1100. General estimate of the costs and times to complete the Supplier Quality Management project?

1101. What lessons were learned about your Supplier Quality Management project management methodology?

1102. Who supplies data?

1103. Does it do what client said it would?

1104. Did the Supplier Quality Management project achieve its MOV?

1105. Do you buy-in installation services?

1106. Was the Supplier Quality Management project goal achieved?

1107. What function(s) does it fill or meet?

1108. What is the Acceptance Management Process?

1109. Is formal acceptance of the Supplier Quality Management project product documented and distributed?

1110. What are the requirements against which to test, Who will execute?

1111. Was the sponsor/customer satisfied?

1112. Who would use it?

1113. What features, practices, and processes proved to be strengths or weaknesses?

1114. Was the client satisfied with the Supplier Quality Management project results?

5.0 Closing Process Group: Supplier Quality Management

1115. Who are the Supplier Quality Management project stakeholders?

1116. When will the Supplier Quality Management project be done?

1117. What were things that you did very well and want to do the same again on the next Supplier Quality Management project?

1118. Can the lesson learned be replicated?

1119. What business situation is being addressed?

1120. Did you do things well?

1121. Based on your Supplier Quality Management project communication management plan, what worked well?

1122. What were the actual outcomes?

1123. What could be done to improve the process?

1124. Are there funding or time constraints?

1125. Did the Supplier Quality Management project team have the right skills?

1126. Were risks identified and mitigated?

1127. Were the outcomes different from the already stated planned?

1128. Is this a follow-on to a previous Supplier Quality Management project?

1129. What areas were overlooked on this Supplier Quality Management project?

5.1 Procurement Audit: Supplier Quality Management

1130. Is there a policy covering the relationship of other departments with vendors?

1131. Are there mechanisms in place to evaluate the performance of the departments suppliers?

1132. Is free and fair (international) competition promoted by organizational policies and legislation, in line with legal, trade organizations and other policies?

1133. Are all claims certified by the officer giving rise to the claim (usually the purchasing agent)?

1134. Does the strategy include a policy for identifying and training suitable procurement staff?

1135. Was a formal review of tenders received undertaken?

1136. Do procedures require cash advances to be returned by transferred or terminated employees before they can receive final paychecks?

1137. Have guidelines incorporating the principles and objectives of a robust procurement practice been established?

1138. Was the estimated contract value in line with the final cost of the contract awarded?

1139. Are approval limits definitive as to amount and classification of expenditure?

1140. Is there a practice that prohibits signing blank purchase orders?

1141. Were standards, certifications and evidence required admissible?

1142. How do you monitor behaviour of procurement staff?

1143. Are proper financing arrangements taken?

1144. Did your organization state the minimum requirements to be met by the variants in the tender documents?

1145. Were all admitted tenderers invited to submit a tender for each specific contract?

1146. Is there no evidence of favouritism towards a particular contractor during the evaluation and negotiation processes?

1147. Are staff members evaluated in accordance with the terms of existing negotiated agreements?

1148. Are checks safeguarded against theft, loss, or misuse?

1149. Can small orders such as magazine subscriptions and non-product items such as membership in organizations be processed by the ordering department?

5.2 Contract Close-Out: Supplier Quality Management

1150. Change in knowledge?

1151. Have all contracts been closed?

1152. Change in attitude or behavior?

1153. Why Outsource?

1154. Are the signers the authorized officials?

1155. Has each contract been audited to verify acceptance and delivery?

1156. Change in circumstances?

1157. Was the contract complete without requiring numerous changes and revisions?

1158. Parties: Authorized?

1159. How/when used ?

1160. Was the contract sufficiently clear so as not to result in numerous disputes and misunderstandings?

1161. Parties: who is involved?

1162. Have all contract records been included in the Supplier Quality Management project archives?

1163. What happens to the recipient of services?

1164. How is the contracting office notified of the automatic contract close-out?

1165. What is capture management?

1166. Have all contracts been completed?

1167. How does it work?

1168. Have all acceptance criteria been met prior to final payment to contractors?

1169. Was the contract type appropriate?

5.3 Project or Phase Close-Out: Supplier Quality Management

1170. If you were the Supplier Quality Management project sponsor, how would you determine which Supplier Quality Management project team(s) and/or individuals deserve recognition?

1171. In preparing the Lessons Learned report, should it reflect a consensus viewpoint, or should the report reflect the different individual viewpoints?

1172. What hierarchical authority does the stakeholder have in your organization?

1173. Who exerted influence that has positively affected or negatively impacted the Supplier Quality Management project?

1174. What are the mandatory communication needs for each stakeholder?

1175. What was learned?

1176. Does the lesson describe a function that would be done differently the next time?

1177. What information is each stakeholder group interested in?

1178. Is the lesson based on actual Supplier Quality Management project experience rather than on independent research?

1179. In addition to assessing whether the Supplier Quality Management project was successful, it is equally critical to analyze why it was or was not fully successful. Are you including this?

1180. What are they?

1181. Is there a clear cause and effect between the activity and the lesson learned?

1182. Planned completion date?

1183. What security considerations needed to be addressed during the procurement life cycle?

1184. How often did each stakeholder need an update?

1185. What advantages do the an individual interview have over a group meeting, and vice-versa?

5.4 Lessons Learned: Supplier Quality Management

1186. How well does the product or service the Supplier Quality Management project produced meet the defined Supplier Quality Management project requirements?

1187. If you had to do this Supplier Quality Management project again, what is the one thing that you would change (related to process, not to technical solutions)?

1188. What is the impact of tax policy on the case?

1189. What Supplier Quality Management project circumstances were not anticipated?

1190. How accurately and timely was the Risk Management Log updated or reviewed?

1191. How much communication is socially oriented?

1192. Was the change control process properly implemented to manage changes to cost, scope, schedule, or quality?

1193. Would you spend your own money to fix this issue?

1194. What is below the surface?

1195. What are your lessons learned that you will keep

in mind for the next Supplier Quality Management project you participate in?

1196. How closely did deliverables match what was defined within the Supplier Quality Management project Scope?

1197. What is the frequency of personal communications?

1198. Do you have any real problems?

1199. Will the information remain current?

1200. Was the purpose of the Supplier Quality Management project, the end products and success criteria clearly defined and agreed at the start?

1201. How effective was the architecture/system design process?

1202. How well defined were the acceptance criteria for Supplier Quality Management project deliverables?

1203. How well do you feel the executives supported this Supplier Quality Management project?

1204. How many government and contractor personnel are authorized for the Supplier Quality Management project?

1205. How useful do individuals find communications?

Index

Made in the USA
Coppell, TX
10 October 2021

63806299R00182